GW00994632

entertaining
with
ANDREW RUDD

DEDICATION

---◆◆◆---

This book is dedicated to my parents, Prue and David Rudd, for their love, support and advice. Not only are they amazing parents, but they are also my true inspiration and my food heroes. They have more integrity than anyone I've ever met and are the light of my life.

MOUTHWATERING RECIPES AND
INSPIRING PARTY IDEAS

entertaining

with

ANDREW
RUDD

Montmolin Press

First published in 2014 by
Montmolin Press
Drury Court, 56–58 Drury Street
Dublin 2
Ireland
www.medley.ie

Hardback   ISBN: 978 1 909483 620
eBook – mobi format   ISBN: 978 1 909483 637
eBook – ePub format   ISBN: 978 1 909483 644

Photography: Harry Weir, assisted by Brian Clarke
Food styling: Paul Arnold and Andrew Rudd
Editor: Lizzie Gore-Grimes
Design: Chenile Keogh
Copy-editor: Robert Doran
Cover design: Design for Writers
Illustrations: Tanya M. Ross
Index: Kate Murphy

Produced by Kazoo Independent Publishing Services
222 Beech Park, Lucan, Co. Dublin
www.kazoopublishing.com

Kazoo Independent Publishing Services is not the publisher of this work. All rights and responsibilities pertaining to this work remain with Montmolin Press.

Kazoo offers independent authors a full range of publishing services. For further details visit www.kazoopublishing.com

Printed in the EU

ACKNOWLEDGEMENTS

---◆◆◆---

I want to thank Paul Arnold for all his hard work over the last couple of years and particularly over the last number of months. Paul was central to the development of this book and provided huge inspiration and support. For this I can't thank him enough. Thanks also to Chris Meyler, my very capable PA. He is my wing commander and has kept the cogs turning over the last two years.

Thanks to Ruth Wassel, the Queen of Demonstrations, for her years of mentoring, advice and encouragement. My first ever cookery demonstration was with Ruth, and we've done many together since. Ruth has provided the inspiration for a great number of my recipes and kindly allowed me to borrow others from her. Without her, I wouldn't have had the confidence to write this book.

To Sinéad Walsh Ryan and Joanne Byrne for their support, friendship and advice. Sinéad, alongside Chris, was instrumental in organising and implementing the PR for this book, which I hope will be the first of many.

To Alina, who has worked with me for many years and has given me great support in developing my business. For this, I am eternally grateful.

To the Irish media for their support over the years, and in particular to Sunshine Radio and TV3, especially Alan Hughes. Also to Victoria O'Brien, Kathy Littler, Bairbre Power, Joe Harrington, Andrea Hayes and Lynsey Dolan, who have all encouraged and supported me.

To Kevin Walsh and his team at Event Waiter, particularly Pat, Cathy, Eoin and Aidan, and to Sonia and Cathy Harris for their continued support and their work on the Domino's Gourmet range and the TV advertising campaign.

To my suppliers, in particular Thomas and Sam Driver, Declan Bagnal, Brian McDonald, Donal Somerville, Mark Patterson of In-House, Mick Smith of Häfele Ireland and Kevin Riordan of Fisher Paykel, Donal and Ciaran of Select Hire, who helped with setting up Medley and its development as a venue. Also to Rosie, Mark and Ollie Shortt for their support over the years.

To Paul, Colm and Chris from The Corkscrew Wine Merchants for recommending the wines to go with the menus in this book and for being so supportive of Medley over the last two years.

To Lizzie Gore-Grimes, Chenile Keogh and Robert Doran, who helped me put the book together.

To my good friend Harry Weir and his assistant, Brian, for the amazing photography. They went above and beyond the call of duty, doing last-minute shoots, touch-ups and revisions, so that everything was perfect. Every minute was a pleasure.

Special thanks to all my friends, for being there through thick and thin. They help me with fun, advice, laughter and, more importantly, naughtiness! You know who you are, but I have to mention Niall, otherwise he "might give me a wide berth"! Now, Niall, happy?

And finally, a huge, heartfelt thank you to all my clients in Medley and in my private catering business. As always, your dish is my command!

CONTENTS

◆◆◆

DINNER FOR TWO

FRIENDS FOR SUPPER

ELEGANT DINNER PARTY

THE BIG FEAST

THE MEDLEY FUSION

BRUNCH AND LONG LAZY LUNCH

DINNER PARTY ON A BUDGET

FOREWORD

◆◆◆

Whenever someone in Ireland does well at something, there are those who will nod sagely and say, "They didn't lick it off the stones," which, for those unfamiliar with the idiom, means that there was some family skill, genetic predisposition or piece of vital information handed down by an ancestor. It's not a put-down, just a way of the commentator affirming that they know the subject's "seed, breed and generation". Still with me? Well, I know a bit about Andrew Rudd and I can say with certainty that he didn't lick it off the stones. He has certainly developed and honed his considerable skills but he inherited a great love of food from his parents, David and Prue, who, back in the seventies, moved to a gothic pile with a leaky roof outside Moneygall, on the main Dublin–Limerick road, and filled it with free-range children and antibiotic-free piggies.

They were friends of a colleague of mine, and when I was travelling on assignments, I would mooch a cup of a tea and exchange recipes and spicy stories with Prue, while David, like the marquis of Blandings, would discourse on the subject of pig breeding and child rearing, very like the character played by Richard Briars in the BBC comedy of the day, *The Good Life*. David even paid the school fees for his brood of nine with consignments of sausages and rashers. Prue developed recipes, notably for puddings and pâtés, while her bucolic brood grew up wonderfully confident, encouraged to develop their own aptitudes in business, the arts and athletics.

Andrew could cook. On top of that he had great communication skills and that showman's flair that meant he was a natural for TV. He is instantly likeable – a Rudd characteristic – and quite presentable too! The important thing for me is that behind the showman and the young man making a career in a tough milieu is a genuinely talented cook who really loves to ply his trade and share his secrets. That's the mark of the real culinary evangelist. Food is for sharing – it's a communion with friends and loved ones. At times food is a feast to celebrate or show off, and Andrew's book has recipes and menus for every occasion from that intimate meal for two, when economy is less of a consideration, to the dinner party, the brunch, the big bash. You can cook this food. You don't need a lot of gimmicky equipment or the skills of a Michelin-starred chef. You require only a spirit of adventure, a love of good food and a copy of Andrew's beautiful book. Enjoy!

Derek Davis
Broadcaster and journalist
October 2014

INTRODUCTION

I grew up, one of nine children, on a pig farm in Moneygall, County Offaly. As you can imagine, with so many siblings, the daily routine of cooking and eating was a huge part of our family life. My mum was twenty-one years old when she married my dad. They moved from Dublin to Moneygall in 1973, the year I was born. In fact I was born a week after we moved. My parents, Prue and David, already had three children, Emma, Ben and Tom, and my dad had two children from a previous marriage, Belinda and Sophie. Even though they are technically half-sisters, they lived with us all our lives, so I consider them absolutely full sisters. While Dad looked after the pigs, Mum was perennially busy cooking and raising her brood of children. Derek Davis, who is a good family friend, once described my parents as terribly hard workers who bred pigs and children, but not necessarily in that order!

We had a half-acre vegetable garden, which meant that we were fairly self-sufficient when it came to food. We also had the pigs, so the fridge and freezer were always full of various cuts of pork. Children tend to get bored easily, so Mum was constantly coming up with new and creative ideas for meals. The children were always called in to help, and that's how my passion for food took flight. In 1985 Mum and Dad launched the Rudd's brand, producing the first commercially available dry-cured Irish bacon and sausages free from antibiotics and growth promoters. At the time, Ireland was experiencing a food revolution, and my parents were considered pioneers as the first people to introduce these artisanal-style products to major supermarkets. Dad had worked with Feargal Quinn in the past, and when they met to discuss the possibility of a listing in Superquinn, Feargal was quick to embrace the brand and the philosophy, which we were very grateful for.

My parents passed on their creative, entrepreneurial spirit to their children. We all still cook, and my brother Simon, my sisters Joanna and Emma and I all work in the food business.

Joanna is the soup queen in the family, and Emma recently started a catering business in Tipperary. Belinda studied with Prue Leith and has worked as a private chef for some very prestigious clients in London and further afield. Sophie has a great ability to throw meals together in seconds. Ben has lived in Paris for years, so he always brings delicious gourmet presents home to Ireland. Tom, who was a National Hunt jockey for years, didn't have quite the same passion for food, as he was constantly trying to keep his weight down. I have to concede that winning the Irish Grand National and the Galway Plate makes up for his "impartial attitude" to food, though! Kate is the only vegetarian in the family, and as an athlete, eating is part of her fitness regime. She has had great success and even competed on the TV show *Gladiators* in the nineties and represented Ireland as a cyclist on many occasions. She probably has the greatest knowledge of nutrition, as it was so important for her sporting career. I guess you could say our love of food is in the blood, and I certainly feel very fortunate to have grown up with such a strong heritage.

As the youngest of the first batch of children, I would spend hours in the kitchen cooking and baking. My poor parents were my guinea pigs, but they put on a brave face. When the second batch came along (Kate, Simon and Joanna), they then became my subjects. Mum had a very clever system to make each of us feel special. She had a "pet calendar" and every week, one of us was the pet, which meant that we got to go shopping with her and lick the bowl when she was making cakes and puddings. She served every meal with homemade bread and pudding, which was always delicious. The best thing about the pet calendar was that for one full week you didn't have to do the washing up. My parents also used to take in foreign students, which meant that we had anything up to twenty for each meal during the summer months. The students came to Ireland to learn English, and were often from fairly well-to-do families in France, Spain and Italy, so their culinary standards were pretty high. Mum embraced the challenge, really letting her creative juices flow, and we had some of the most amazing meals.

After school I went InterRailing around Europe. I guess this was another significant inspiration for me and it developed my fascination with food even more. After a month, I ended up on the Greek island of Syros, where I worked for two months in a private villa. My sister Emma was the cook and I was the everything-else guy: gardener, bed maker, painter, floor cleaner, etc. One of my jobs was to do all the food shopping every morning after breakfast. I would drive to the local town on a quad bike and buy from the local markets. I built up a great relationship with all of the stallholders, using my limited Greek. Laden down with groceries and booze, I would then head back to help my sister make lunch. I remember diving for sea urchins was a real highlight. I returned the following summer to work as a chef with my friend Alannah and we had such fun. It was during that time that my love of food really blossomed and the foundations were laid for the career I would later embark on. This inspired me to go on and study agricultural marketing at Harper Adams University and then to do a master's degree in agricultural economics, both of which introduced an element of structure for my future career.

Today my mum works with me in Medley at least twice a week. She has a natural instinct when it comes to food, and the idea of having forty guests for dinner doesn't faze her in the slightest. Whenever we have events in Medley I introduce the staff, one by one, to our guests. I introduce Mum last, and she always gets an incredible reception from the guests. At sixty-eight, she continues to be a pillar of strength and a source of endless inspiration to me.

XII

Andrew Rudd
October 2014

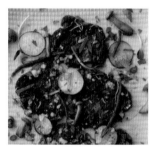

DINNER FOR TWO

❖

These recipes are for those occasions when you're making an effort to impress that special someone or perhaps just treating a good friend. This is when we splash out on ingredients that we might not otherwise buy. It's also a great excuse to experiment with some more involved dishes, such as the monkfish with crab and lobster bisque on page 25 or classic French tarte tatin on page 37. The recipes in this chapter are not difficult but they do impress. I like to think of this kind of food as fine dining in the comfort of your own home. If you want to push the boat out, it's a lovely idea to serve two small starters, followed by a main course and dessert. Or alternatively you could prepare two desserts and serve a tasting plate of each one for that extra wow factor. You'll notice some of these recipes serve more than two, which means there will be plenty of leftovers to enjoy the next day!

OYSTERS ROCKEFELLER

◆◆◆

This dish consists of oysters on the half-shell that have been topped with some delicious ingredients and then baked. It was created in 1840 at a restaurant in New Orleans called Antoine's. We used Clew Bay Oysters in Medley last year for the launch party of the Westport Festival of Music and Food. I wanted to serve fresh oysters on the night, but I also wanted to do something a little different. This recipe is the result of my experimentation.

prep: 5 minutes ◆ **cook**: 10 minutes ◆ **serves**: 2

FOR THE OYSTERS

6 small fresh oysters

250ml cream

250ml milk

salt and freshly cracked black pepper

nutmeg

FOR THE CRUMB TOPPING

35g breadcrumbs (roughly 1 slice of bread)

1 tsp chilli powder

1 tbsp finely chopped flat leaf parsley

salt and freshly cracked black pepper

FOR THE SHALLOT SAUCE

100g butter

2 shallots, peeled and finely diced

3 garlic cloves, peeled and finely chopped

salt and freshly cracked black pepper

100ml white wine

100ml vegetable stock

100g baby spinach (uncooked)

TO SERVE

1 lemon, cut into wedges

Tabasco sauce (optional)

Preheat the grill.

Shuck the oysters and remove the top shell. Place the oysters, in their natural juices, in a large saucepan with the cream and milk. Season with salt, pepper and nutmeg. Bring up the heat and simmer gently for 1–2 minutes. Remove the oysters from the creamy mixture and drain. Place the oysters in the shell on a baking tray lined with parchment paper.

Prepare the topping by combining the breadcrumbs with the chilli powder and flat leaf parsley in a bowl and seasoning with salt and pepper.

Place a pan over a medium heat and add the butter. Once it begins to foam, sauté the shallots and garlic. Season with salt and pepper and add the wine and stock. Cook over a high heat for 2 minutes, and then reduce the heat and simmer for 5 minutes. Add the spinach and cook for a further minute. Remove from the heat.

Spoon just enough of the shallot mixture on top of each oyster shell to cover the poached oyster. Sprinkle a little breadcrumb mixture over the shallot and repeat for each oyster.

Place under the grill for approximately 2 minutes or until the breadcrumb topping has turned a light golden brown. Serve immediately with sliced lemon and Tabasco sauce.

◆◆◆

CHEF'S TIP

◆ The shallot sauce needs to be well reduced so that it's not too thin.

SEARED CARPACCIO OF BEEF WITH CHILLI, GINGER AND SOY SAUCE

───── ❖❖❖ ─────

This is a really easy dish to prepare. Not only does it look like art on the plate, but it's also sophisticated, decadent, elegant and above all fragrant. You won't need to slice the entire fillet here but you need the larger piece to be able to slice it. The rest of the beef can be used the following day for a roast joint.

prep: 10–15 minutes ✦ **serves**: 2–4

500g fillet of beef

salt and freshly cracked black pepper

1 tbsp butter

10 small chanterelle mushrooms

2 radishes, thinly sliced

1 tbsp very finely sliced or grated fresh ginger

½ red chilli, deseeded and finely sliced

½ green chilli, deseeded and finely sliced

1 tbsp of chopped fresh coriander

toasted sesame seed oil

soy sauce

juice of 1 lime

TO SERVE

handful of fresh coriander, roughly chopped

fresh samphire, blanched in boiling water for 30 seconds and then plunged into ice-cold water (optional)

Season the beef fillet with salt and pepper. Heat half of the butter in a large frying pan and sear the beef until the meat is browned on all sides (about 3 minutes per side). Remove from the pan and allow to rest.

In the meantime, sauté the mushrooms in the remaining butter until golden. This should take no more than 3 minutes over a high heat. Season with salt and pepper. Remove from the heat and transfer to kitchen paper to soak up any surplus butter. Allow to cool.

Slice the beef as thinly as you can and lay the slices on a platter. Two slices per person is more than sufficient.

Arrange the sliced radish on the platter, followed by the mushrooms. Feel free to be creative at this point. Sprinkle the finely sliced or grated ginger and the sliced chilli over. Drizzle over a small amount of sesame oil, soy sauce and lime juice. Use circular movements from a height to make sure each slice of beef gets an equal amount. Taste, and add more lime juice, if needed. Finally garnish with chopped fresh coriander (or parsley if you prefer) and a scattering of samphire (optional).

───── ❖❖❖ ─────

CHEF'S TIPS

✦ If you are doing this for a dinner party, the beef can be seared and the ingredients prepared well in advance, but combine the ingredients just before serving, as the lime juice cooks the beef.

✦ To spice things up even more, try adding some crushed coriander seeds and fresh thyme when you are seasoning the beef at the beginning of the recipe.

FRENCH ONION SOUP

The key to this recipe is to cook the onions slowly until they become caramelised. Throughout history, onion soup was seen as peasant food because onions were cheap, plentiful and easy to grow. The modern version of this soup originated in France in the eighteenth century and uses beef stock as its base. It can be difficult to find a good French onion soup recipe, but I can certainly stand by this version. As this recipe serves more than two, you can enjoy the leftovers the next day.

prep: 10 minutes ✦ **cook**: 65 minutes ✦ **serves**: 4–6

2 tbsp olive oil

70g butter

750g onions (about 3 medium onions), sliced

3 garlic cloves, finely chopped

1 litre rich beef stock (made with 1 litre water and 4 beef stock cubes)

200ml white wine

1 tbsp sugar

salt and freshly cracked black pepper

TO SERVE

baguette, sliced and toasted

Gruyère cheese, grated

In a large heavy-based pan (casserole or similar), heat the oil and the butter. Once the butter has melted, add the onions and garlic and sauté over a high heat for 5 minutes. Reduce the heat and leave to sauté gently for 20 minutes.

It's important to cook the onions slowly and to stir them frequently. The key is to allow the flavours to come out, which will happen as the onions begin to brown and caramelise.

Add the stock, wine and sugar and season with salt and pepper. Increase the heat and allow to boil for 5 minutes, and then reduce the heat and simmer for a further 35 minutes.

If you like, you can pop some slices of baguette topped with Gruyère cheese under the grill until the cheese is melted and golden brown. Serve the soup with one or two of these toasted cheese croutons on top.

CHEF'S TIPS

✦ Use a very good beef stock as this intensifies the flavour. I generally double the concentration of stock and use 4 stock cubes for the 1 litre required.

✦ A dash of cognac will add great flavour too.

✦ The longer you cook the soup, the more liquid will evaporate. Just be careful to take this into account so that you don't run out when serving.

SEARED SCALLOPS WITH BLACK PUDDING AND PEA AND MINT PURÉE

◆◆◆

The combination of peas and fresh mint is a match made in heaven. This dish is guaranteed to impress your guest! Scallops are sweet, creamy, incredibly elegant and really quick to cook. You just need to make sure you get them nicely seared on the outside and yet lovely and tender and moist inside. This dish also works really well as a canapé — simply serve the black pudding topped with the scallops, and then drizzle over the infused butter followed by a little of the pea and mint purée and add a small mint leaf to garnish.

prep: 10 minutes ◆ **cook**: 20 minutes ◆ **serves**: 2

FOR THE PEA AND MINT PURÉE

50g butter

½ shallot, finely chopped

1 garlic clove, peeled and chopped

salt and freshly cracked black pepper

200g frozen peas

20ml vegetable stock

2 tsp finely chopped fresh mint (at least 6 leaves)

pinch of sugar

FOR THE SCALLOPS

4 fresh large scallops

30ml extra virgin olive oil

salt and freshly cracked black pepper

50g butter

TO SERVE

4 slices black pudding, about 2cm thick

baby salad leaves, washed

sprigs of fresh mint

Preheat the oven to 70°C fan/90°C/gas mark ¼.

Pan-fry the black pudding over a medium heat until crisp and browned on both sides. Then transfer to the preheated oven. This will only take about 4 minutes, as black pudding is generally precooked when you buy it.

To make the pea and mint purée, place a medium-sized saucepan over a medium heat and melt the butter. Then add the shallot and garlic. Season with salt and pepper and sauté until the shallot becomes translucent but does not brown. Add the peas and pour over the stock. Bring to the boil, then reduce the heat and simmer for 10 minutes. Add the fresh mint and then blend the liquid in a food processor or using a hand blender. Taste, and check the seasoning. Add a pinch of sugar to enhance the flavour. This purée can be served warm or cold and has the right consistency to brush onto the plate as a garnish.

To prepare the scallops, first rinse them in cold water, making sure not to remove the coral. Dry well on absorbent kitchen paper and then sprinkle them with salt and pepper and drizzle over some olive oil. Melt the butter in a heavy-based frying pan over a medium heat. Do not let the butter burn. When it is just foaming, add the scallops to the pan and cook them for 1½ minutes (if small) to 2 minutes (if large) on each side or until golden brown. Remove from the heat and keep warm (by covering with foil or placing them in the oven pre-heated to 70°C fan/90°C/gas mark ¼). Retain the butter and cooking liquid from the pan, as this will be used as the dressing.

To serve, using a pastry brush, brush a thick line of pea and mint purée down the centre of the plate (about 3cm wide) from top to bottom. Assemble the salad leaves in the centre, heaped neatly. Place 2 scallops and 2 pieces of the black pudding on the leaves. Dress with 1 tablespoon of the retained butter from the frying pan, and garnish with a sprig of fresh mint.

Serve immediately.

MONKFISH WITH CRAB AND LOBSTER BISQUE

◆◆◆

Monkfish is a meaty fish with beautifully firm flesh that doesn't break up after cooking. However, the fillet will lose liquid as it cooks (you will notice a milky substance oozing out) and this reduces the size of the fillet, so it's a good idea to buy large ones. The marinade really does enhance the flavour of the fillets and you don't have to season before cooking, as there is salt and pepper in the marinade. This is a sumptuous and luxurious recipe that is quick and easy to prepare. The bisque is divine and could also be served on the side in a small shot glass. Yummy!

prep: 10 minutes ◆ **marinate**: 30 minutes or overnight ◆ **cook**: 35 minutes ◆ **serves**: 2

2 monkfish centre fillets (about 200g each), well trimmed

FOR THE MARINADE

100ml extra virgin olive oil

1 tbsp chopped fresh tarragon

½ tsp salt

½ tsp freshly cracked black pepper

FOR THE BISQUE

1 tbsp olive oil

1 tsp crushed garlic

1 tsb grated ginger

1 roasted red papper (see page 229)

1 small shallot, finely diced

250ml chicken stock or fish stock

1 lobster stock cube or 100g cooked lobster meat

50ml white wine

pinch of sugar

100g cooked crabmeat (pasteurised)

½ tsp red food colouring

salt and freshly cracked black pepper

◆◆◆

CHEF'S TIP

✦ The bisque can be prepared in advance and kept in the fridge for up to 4 days before serving.

To prepare the marinade, simply combine all the ingredients in a bowl (or large ziplock bag) and whisk them together thoroughly or blitz for a few seconds in a food processor. Place the monkfish fillets in the marinade, turn them over in the liquid to make sure they are well coated and cover the bowl (or seal the bag). Refrigerate for at least 30 minutes, or overnight if possible.

To prepare the bisque, heat the oil in a pan, add the garlic, ginger, shallot, roasted red pepper and lightly sauté for 5 minutes over a medium heat. Season with a little salt and pepper. Add the stock, lobster stock cube (or lobster meat), white wine and sugar. Bring to the boil and add the crabmeat. Then reduce the heat and simmer gently for 10 minutes. Add the red food colouring. Using a hand blender, blend until smooth. Taste and season with salt and pepper, if needed. Note that the stock is already salty so be careful not to overdo it on the salt. Keep warm before serving.

Preheat the oven to 180°C fan/200°C/gas mark 6.

Remove the monkfish fillets from the marinade, drain and pat dry with kitchen paper. Seal them on a hot griddle pan for about 2–3 minutes on each side. Then transfer the fillets to a wire rack placed on top of a baking tray and cook in the hot oven for 10 minutes. The tray will catch the excess cooking juices from the fish. Remove from the oven and allow to rest for 3 minutes before serving. Cover with tinfoil to keep warm.

Serve immediately with the bisque and your choice of seasonal vegetables.

HONEY ROASTED DUCK BREASTS WITH SPICED PUY LENTILS AND CARAMELISED APPLES

❖❖❖

When you're cooking duck it's critical to render the fat out of the duck breast in order to make the duck beautifully succulent. The combination of the puy lentils and the caramelised apples in this dish produces a fusion of subtle but complex flavours.

prep: 10 minutes ✦ **cook**: 55 minutes ✦ **serves**: 2

FOR THE DUCK

2 duck breasts, skin on

salt and freshly cracked black pepper

50ml honey

FOR THE PUY LENTILS

½ red onion, peeled and finely diced

1 garlic clove, finely chopped

½ red chilli

½ tsp grated fresh ginger

½ tsp ground ginger

½ tsp ground paprika

½ tsp ground cloves

50ml olive oil

1 tbsp boiling water

50g butter

200g puy lentils

100ml red wine

½ tbsp soy sauce

150ml vegetable stock

1 tbsp chopped fresh coriander

zest and juice of ½ lime

Score the duck breasts with a sharp knife and season with salt and pepper. Place a shallow frying pan over a high heat and pour the honey into the pan. When it starts to bubble, add the duck breasts skin side down, reduce the heat to medium and cook for about 6–8 minutes to let the fat render out. Then turn the breasts over to brown on the other side for about 30 seconds.

Remove the breasts from the pan and transfer to a baking tray. Discard the juices.

To prepare the lentils, place the onion, garlic, chilli, ginger, paprika and cloves into a blender. Add the olive oil and 1 tablespoon of boiling water. Blend to a smooth paste.

In a pan, fry the paste in the butter for 3 minutes over a high heat. Add the lentils, wine and soy sauce and 100ml of vegetable stock and cook over a medium heat for 35 minutes or until cooked (when you bite into them they should be soft but not mushy). If the mixture looks like it's drying out just add more stock as needed. Add the coriander, lime juice and zest and stir to combine. Taste, and season with salt, pepper and sugar as needed.

Preheat the oven to 180°C fan/200°C/gas mark 6.

Arrange the duck breasts skin side up on the baking tray, cover with tin foil and place in the oven on the middle shelf. If you place a dish of water on the bottom shelf, the steam will help to keep the duck moist. Cook for about 15 minutes (for medium) or until cooked to your liking (see my guide below). Remove

Continued overleaf

pinch sugar

salt and freshly cracked black pepper

FOR THE CARAMELISED APPLES

1 Bramley apple, peeled and cored

25g butter

zest and juice of ½ lemon

1 tbsp caster sugar

½ tbsp sweet liqueur, such as Grand
  Marnier

TO SERVE

½ red chilli, finely sliced

½ green chilli, finely sliced

fresh coriander, chopped

chicken jus (see recipe on page 212)

from the oven and allow to rest for 4 minutes, keeping them covered in tin foil and in a warm place.

For the caramelised apples, cut the peeled and cored apples into large segments. Place the butter in a shallow frying pan. Add the apples, sugar, lemon zest and juice, and lightly fry for 1 minute. Add the liqueur. Continue cooking for a further 1–2 minutes. Remove from the heat. Allow to cool.

To serve, slice the duck breasts and place in the centre of the plate. On one side, fan 4 segments of apple and on the other side, spoon a portion of the puy lentils. Finish with a drizzle of chicken jus if you like (see recipe on page 212).

Garnish with a sprinkle of chopped fresh chilli and coriander.

CHEF'S TIPS

+ To get really crispy skin on your duck breasts, place them skin side down in a cold pan over a medium heat and cook for 6–8 minutes or until golden brown. Pour the fat off regularly. Cook on the other side for 30 seconds, to seal. Then simply transfer to the oven for the required cooking time.

> rare: 10 minutes
>
> medium: 15 minutes
>
> well done: 18 minutes

+ By properly cooking duck, you can eliminate 70 per cent of the fat, which leaves a delicious, crisp skin that adds to the distinct flavour of the meat.

+ Ensure that the skin and flesh of the duck breasts are dry, before scoring with a very sharp knife. Then season well with natural sea salt and pepper. When you are roasting meat, the skin should always be as dry as possible to ensure you get a crispy finish.

+ Always cook skin side down first, so the fat has a chance to render, or melt out of the skin.

MEDALLIONS OF LAMB CANNON WITH A CORIANDER AND MINT SALSA

◆◆◆

The first time that I had lamb cannon was in Istanbul. I was doing a show with Alan Hughes for TV3's Ireland AM. *We visited Mikla restaurant and interviewed Mehmet Gürs. The menu had a Turkish–Scandinavian feel that reflected Mehmet's background. He gave me a masterclass in his kitchen, and the dish we did was lamb cannon, which was gently sealed and roasted in the oven for only 4 minutes. This is a stunning dish with a beautiful salsa, which I've borrowed from my friend Ruth Wassel.*

prep: 15 minutes ◆ **marinate**: 24 hours ◆ **cook**: 8 minutes ◆ **serves**: 2

1 lamb cannon (or you can use 1 pork steak), trimmed

FOR THE MARINADE

2 tsp coriander seeds

1 tsp cumin seeds

3 black peppercorns

¼ tsp Maldon sea salt

1 garlic clove

1 tbsp red wine vinegar

3 tbsp olive oil

FOR THE CORIANDER AND MINT SALSA

2 garlic cloves, crushed

1 anchovy fillet, roughly chopped

1 tsp lemon zest

1 tbsp lemon juice

80ml extra virgin olive oil

freshly cracked salt and pepper

1 tbsp chopped fresh coriander leaves

1 tbsp chopped fresh mint leaves

TO SERVE

creamy mash (see recipe on page 98)

selection of seasonal vegetables

To make the marinade, dry fry the coriander seeds, cumin seeds, peppercorns and salt over a high heat for 30 seconds, to release their flavour. Add this spice mix to the garlic in a pestle and mortar and crush to a paste. Stir in the vinegar and then the oil. Put the lamb cannon in a large plastic ziplock bag and pour in the marinade. Coat evenly and marinate for a few hours or overnight if you can.

To make the salsa, mash the crushed garlic and anchovy together in a small bowl and add the lemon zest and juice. Season with salt and pepper and stir in the oil and fresh herbs. Alternatively, blitz in a food processor.

Preheat the oven to 180°C fan/200°C/gas mark 4.

To cook the lamb, place an ovenproof frying pan over a high heat and lightly oil it. You can also use a dollop of butter for extra flavour. Then add the lamb to the pan and brown the meat on all sides to seal in the flavour. Retain the marinade. Baste with a spoon or a pastry brush, using the retained marinade and butter. This will take about 2 minutes. Transfer the pan to the oven for 8 minutes or until the lamb is cooked through. Allow to rest for 4 minutes.

Slice the lamb cannon to your desired thickness (around 2cm is fine), and serve with the salsa, on a bed of mashed potatoes (see recipe on page 98) and seasonal vegetables.

FILLET OF BEEF

———————— ❖ ————————

This is one of the easiest ways of serving something really special, relatively quickly. But please don't overcook the beef as you will lose the succulence and tender flavour. If you follow the preparation and cooking times below, you will have the perfect main course to serve your guests who will be salivating in anticipation. The quality of the beef is important, so do ask your butcher for an aged fillet.

prep: 1 hour ✦ **marinate**: 2–24 hours ✦ **cook**: 20–50 minutes ✦ **serves**: 6

FOR THE BEEF

1kg beef fillet, well trimmed

50ml olive oil

FOR THE PEPPER CRUST

2 tbsp peppercorns

2 tbsp coriander seeds

1 tbsp rock salt

bunch of fresh thyme

FOR THE JUS

100g cold unsalted butter, cubed

2 shallots, peeled and finely diced

1 tbsp chopped fresh thyme

2 garlic cloves, crushed

freshly cracked salt and pepper

500ml concentrated beef stock
(homemade or made using 2 beef stock
cubes)

1 tbsp balsamic vinegar

150ml Madeira wine or red wine

To prepare the beef, trim the fillet to remove any sinew, outer layers of fat or white membrane.

In a large pan, dry fry the peppercorns and coriander seeds for the pepper crust. You just want to toast them gently to release their flavour. Be careful not to burn them or to allow the pan to smoke. Remove them from the heat and crush with a pestle and mortar. Then add the salt and thyme and mix well. Spread the mixture out on a flat tray.

Into a flat dish, pour a generous amount (50ml) of olive oil. Roll the beef fillet in the olive oil and then roll it in the pepper crust mixture. Continue until the fillet is evenly covered in a thin layer of spice crust. Tightly wrap the crusted fillet in cling film and then in tin foil. Place in the fridge overnight or for a minimum of 2 hours. Make sure to remove the beef from the fridge at least one hour before you are going to cook it, to allow it to come back up to room temperature.

To prepare the jus, sauté the shallots, thyme and garlic in 50g of the butter. Season with salt and pepper. Add the stock, balsamic vinegar and Madeira wine, bring up to the boil and then reduce to a simmer. Let the jus gently simmer until the liquid has reduced in volume by half. Remove from the heat. Check the seasoning and add more salt and pepper, if desired. After the beef has been cooked, make sure to add the juices to the jus. Then gently heat the sauce and whisk in the remaining 50g of cubed butter, until the butter is melted. You can also strain the jus to remove the shallots and garlic if you like. Personally, I prefer the texture of the jus with the finely chopped shallots.

Continued overleaf

Preheat the oven to 200°C fan/220°C/gas mark 7.

To cook the beef, heat a non-stick frying pan with a little vegetable oil in it. When it is very hot, add the beef and sear it on all sides for 1½–2 minutes on each side until evenly browned all over. Place in a roasting tin.

Place the roasting tin in the oven for 12 minutes for rare, 20 minutes for medium rare, 30 for medium, or 45 minutes for well done. Remove from the oven. Cover with a damp tea towel and then tin foil and allow to rest in a warm oven (65–70°C) for at least 5 minutes before carving (rare). There is a rule of thumb that the resting time should be half the cooking time.

To serve, slice the beef (not too thick) into about 20 slices. Drizzle the jus over and around the meat. Serve with a selection of seasonal vegetables. Baby potatoes and asparagus are particularly good with this dish.

CHEF'S TIPS

+ I recommend cooking the beef rare. Once sliced, the hot jus poured over the beef will continue to cook it and it won't look as rare as you might expect.

+ Another way to work out cooking times is with a temperature probe. You simply insert it into the thickest part of the beef joint and it will give you a reading.

> 60°C is rare
>
> 70°C is medium
>
> 80°C is well done

+ The resting period is a critical element in cooking meat. The fibres in meat tighten up during cooking and resting allows them to relax again.

TARTE TATIN

◆◆◆

Tarte tatin is an upside-down tart, where the fruit is caramelised in butter and sugar before the tart is baked. In Medley we were recently devising a new French menu for our cookery classes, and my chef Paul came up with six different variations of this classic dessert. This is the one we settled on. It is truly delicious. As this recipe serves more than two, you can enjoy the leftovers the next day.

prep: 15 minutes ✦ **chill**: 24 hours ✦ **cook**: 25 minutes ✦ **serves**: 8–12

90g butter

180g caster sugar

1 shot (30ml) Aperol or similar liqueur (optional)

5–6 dessert apples (Cox's or Granny Smith), peeled, cored and sliced

450g puff pastry

beaten-egg, to glaze

◆◆◆

CHEF'S TIPS

✦ The pastry base is really not that important. Quite unusually for a French recipe, you are given a certain amount of freedom to use a pastry of your choice on top of the apples. Larousse's recipe specifies shortcrust but concedes that "alternatively puff pastry can be used". We prefer the puff pastry version.

✦ Cooking apples are tasty but go mushy when cooked and do not work with this recipe, as they don't hold their shape. Cox's or Granny Smiths are perfect.

If you can, place the prepared apples in the fridge, drizzled with lemon juice to prevent them from discolouring, uncovered, for 24 hours, as this will help them to stay firmer and plumper when cooked.

In a deep, ovenproof, heavy-bottomed frying pan (about 28cm diameter x 4cm depth), melt the butter and add the sugar. Cook until golden brown. Add the Aperol (or similar liqueur) and cook off the alcohol for about 30 seconds to 1 minute.

Arrange the apple slices in the base of the pan in overlapping circles, working from the outside into the centre. Keep the arrangement nice and tight, as the layer of apples will be the top of your tart once it is cooked and turned out.

Preheat the oven to 180°C fan/200°C/gas mark 6.

Caramelise the apples in the pan for about 10 minutes over a medium heat, until they are slightly soft when pressed down. The liquid should be quite dark in colour, similar to toffee.

Roll out the puff pastry on a floured surface until it is about 2–3cm greater in diameter than the pan. Lay the pastry over the apples in the pan and push the edges down the side of the pan so they will form a ridge around the tart.

Glaze the top with a little beaten-egg and prick all over with a fork so the pastry doesn't puff up when cooking.

Bake in the hot oven for 25 minutes. When the tart is cooked, leave it to settle in the frying pan for 5 minutes or so before running the blade of a knife round the edge to dislodge any pastry that has stuck. Invert a plate over the top and turn out the tart, along with any juices left in the pan.

Serve with softly whipped cream.

TIRAMISU

✦✦✦

This is one of my favourite desserts. I always order tiramisu if it's on the menu. I'm fascinated by how other chefs make this dish, and I have tried many variations. This recipe has the right balance of coffee and liqueur for me. It's important that you don't overpower the subtle flavours with too much coffee or liqueur. It's also important not to make it too sweet. As this recipe serves more than two, you can enjoy the leftovers the next day.

prep: 30 minutes ✦ **chill**: 24 hours ✦ **serves**: 6

2 free-range egg whites

250ml cream

4 free-range egg yolks

1 tbsp vanilla extract

150g caster sugar

250g mascarpone

200g sponge fingers (approx. 24)

250ml freshly brewed coffee

50ml Grand Marnier liqueur, or similar

6 gelatine sheets (1 gelatine leaf is equivalent to 1 tsp of powdered gelatine)

120g good quality dark chocolate, grated

TO SERVE

cocoa powder, to dust

YOU WILL ALSO NEED

23cm x 23cm x 5cm square serving dish, or similar, lined with cling film

Whisk the egg whites in a clean, dry bowl until they form stiff peaks. In a separate bowl, whisk the cream.

In a small Pyrex bowl, beat the egg yolks, vanilla extract and sugar, and then place the bowl over a saucepan of simmering water (creating a bain-marie) and cook over a low heat for 5 minutes, stirring continuously. Remove the Pyrex bowl from the bain-marie and allow to cool for 5 minutes.

Fold together all the ingredients, including mascarpone, in the bowl containing the whipped egg whites. Add 20ml of the liqueur.

Prepare the sheets of gelatine by soaking in a bowl of cold water for 5 minutes, allowing them to swell slightly. Remove from the water and gently squeeze out any excess liquid. Place the gelatine in a small saucepan with 100ml of the mascarpone cream mixture. Gently heat until completely dissolved. Through a small sieve, strain this back into the mascarpone cream mixture. Gently whisk to combine.

Pour the coffee and the remaining liqueur into a small shallow dish and dip the sponge fingers into this liquid. Then carefully make a layer of them in the base of your tiramisu serving dish, one by one until the base is covered. This should use half your sponge fingers.

Spread half the mascarpone cream onto the sponge fingers and then sprinkle with half the grated chocolate. (If you're looking for perfect presentation, you can refrigerate for 20 minutes at this stage and again after you've added the second layer of the sponge fingers.) Repeat the layers once more in the same order – soaked sponge fingers, mascarpone cream, grated chocolate. Cover and refrigerate overnight.

Sprinkle with cocoa powder before serving.

PANNA COTTA WITH CARDAMOM

Panna cotta simply means "cooked cream" in Italian, and so this dessert can be in danger of being a little bland when it's made in the traditional way. That's why I like to add cardamom, which works beautifully to enhance the flavour. The texture and taste of this dish is very similar to a dessert I found years ago in Keith Floyd's Floyd on Britain and Ireland. *I've since sadly lost the book but this recipe deserves a toast to Keith Floyd, who was my inspiration when I was growing up.*

prep: 30 minutes ✦ **chill**: 24 hours ✦ **serves**: 6

250ml full-fat milk

250ml double cream

1 vanilla pod, split lengthways with seeds scraped out

½ tsp cardamom powder, available in good delis and Asian markets

7 cardamom pods, seeds removed, toasted and crushed

30g caster sugar

2 heaped tsp gelatine powder or 12g sachet, plus 50ml boiling water

YOU WILL ALSO NEED

5 x 100ml ramekins (5.5cm x 5.5cm)

To a small saucepan add the milk, cream, vanilla pod and seeds, cardamom powder, cardamom seeds and sugar, and bring to a simmer. This will take about 5 minutes. Remove from the heat and allow the flavours to infuse for 10 minutes.

To dissolve the gelatine, pour 50ml of boiling water into a bowl. Add the gelatine to the hot water, not the other way round. Stir until the gelatine has dissolved. Pour into the milk mixture and stir well.

Strain the mix through a fine sieve to remove the vanilla pod and the cardamom seeds. This will also remove any gelatine that has not fully dissolved.

Divide the mixture between five ramekins and leave to cool. Refrigerate for at least an hour, but overnight is better.

CHEF'S TIP

✦ If you can't find any cardamom powder, just use an additional 5 pods (12 in total). Complement the subtle flavour of this panna cotta with some fresh berries.

DINNER FOR TWO

FRENCH BISTRO

French onion soup
Fillet of beef
Tarte tatin

Wine suggestions
White:an Alsatian Pinot Gris ✦ Red: a good level Chianti Classico

INDULGENT DELIGHTS

Seared scallops with black pudding and pea and mint purée
Honey roasted duck breasts with spiced puy lentils and caramelised apples
Tiramisu

Wine suggestions
White: a nice Pinot blanc from France or Germany ✦ Red: a medium- to full-bodied Syrah or Grenache from the south of France

LIGHT AND ELEGANT

Seared carpaccio of beef with chilli, ginger and soy sauce
Monkfish with crab and lobster bisque
Panna cotta with cardamom

Wine suggestions
White: an unoaked Burgundy Chardonnay ✦ Red: a soft, juicy Cabernet Franc from the Loire Valley

FRIENDS FOR
SUPPER

◆◆◆

This is easy entertaining at its best. The recipes in this chapter are ideal for a casual gathering, when you're having four to six people over. It's full of ideas for food that is fresh, quick and easy to prepare, and most importantly, full of flavour. This is without doubt my favourite way to entertain. The recipes in this chapter are very accessible and won't put too much pressure on you in the kitchen. Many of them can be prepared in advance. I also love the idea of simply placing platters and casserole dishes on the table and letting guests help themselves. With this kind of an evening there's no need for the formality of fussy plating.

GREEK SALAD

The traditional Greek salad is one of the most vibrant salads I have ever tasted. When I was a student I worked on a small Greek Island called Syros for two summer seasons. I probably had this every day for lunch and I never tired of it. I still haven't. The key to this salad lies in using the finest ingredients.

prep: 10 minutes ✦ **serves**: 8

2 packets (about 400g) best quality feta cheese

2 tbsp dried oregano

extra virgin olive oil

500g cherry tomatoes

1 cucumber

6 spring onions

1 small red onion

12–18 Kalamata olives, pitted

juice of ½ lemon

salt and freshly cracked black pepper

sugar to taste

TO SERVE

flat leaf parsley

Chop the feta into cubes and place in a shallow bowl. Sprinkle over the dried oregano and drizzle generously with extra virgin olive oil. Cover and transfer to the fridge to marinate while you prepare the rest of the salad.

Slice the tomatoes in half. Chop the cucumber into large cubes, leaving the skin on. Chop the spring onion coarsely, and dice the red onion very finely. Put these into a bowl with the olives. Drizzle with olive oil and lemon juice and add salt, pepper and sugar to taste. Add in the feta cheese, toss gently and garnish with some sprigs of flat leaf parsley.

CHEF'S TIP

✦ The feta can be left in the fridge to marinate for a couple of hours; this will only improve the flavour. However, it will need to be left out to come up to room temperature for at least 1 hour before serving. The salad should be dressed only at the last minute or it will go soggy.

MOZZARELLA AND PARMA HAM WITH A CHILLI, GARLIC AND OLIVE DRESSING

❖

This is a simple recipe that can be modified to include vine-ripened tomatoes, grilled peppers and sliced red onions. If you leave out the Parma ham, this also works beautifully as a vegetarian dish.

prep: 10 minutes ✦ **serves**: 6

FOR THE DRESSING

3 garlic cloves, crushed

sea salt and freshly ground black pepper, to taste

2 chillies, finely chopped

12 black olives, pitted and finely chopped

zest of 1 unwaxed lemon

150ml extra virgin olive oil

FOR THE SALAD

handful fresh rocket or baby salad leaves

2 x 125g buffalo mozzarella balls

6 slices Parma ham

6 quail eggs, plus 150ml red wine vinegar (this helps to remove the shell from the quail eggs)

To make the dressing, put the crushed garlic and sea salt in a bowl or a pestle and mortar and mix well to produce a pulp. Add the chillies, olives, lemon zest and olive oil and mix to combine. Season with pepper. Allow to sit for up to 30 minutes. The flavours will develop and may require adjustment.

Fill a small saucepan with water and bring to the boil. With a slotted spoon, lower the quail eggs into the boiling water so that they are fully immersed. Boil for exactly 2 minutes over a high heat. After 2 minutes remove the eggs and immediately immerse them in ice-cold water. This will stop them from cooking any further. After 3 minutes, remove the eggs from the water and carefully place them in a small bowl. Cover with red wine vinegar and allow to soak for 2 minutes. Then return them to the cold water and carefully remove the shells.

Scatter some fresh rocket or baby salad leaves over a large platter and arrange slices of mozzarella and Parma ham on top. Then add the quail eggs. Drizzle the dressing over the salad just before serving.

CHEF'S TIP

❖ You can replace the large mozzarella balls with mini mozzarella balls, known as bocconcini. They have a spongy texture and absorb flavour really well.

SPICED BUTTERNUT SQUASH SOUP

This is a lovely recipe for all sorts of occasions. It works particularly well at Christmas, or you can serve it in shot glasses as a canapé.

prep: 20 minutes ✦ **cook**: 20 minutes ✦ **serves**: 6–8

1 butternut squash, about 1.5kg

2 garlic cloves, peeled

1 tbsp olive oil

50g butter

2 onions, diced

salt and freshly cracked black pepper

1 tsp curry power

1 tsp Thai curry paste (optional)

1.5 litres vegetable stock

100ml cream

FOR THE SPICE MIX

½ tsp whole cumin seeds

½ tsp whole coriander seeds

½ tsp black peppercorns

150g butter

1 stick cinnamon

1 tsp white mustard seeds

Preheat the oven to 200° fan/220°C/gas mark 7.

Cut the butternut squash in half lengthwise. Scoop out the seeds and membrane and transfer to a roasting dish. Drizzle with olive oil and roast with the garlic in the oven for 15 minutes. Remove and allow to cool. Scoop out the now soft flesh and set aside with the roasted garlic cloves.

Add the butter to a heavy-bottomed pan over a medium heat. Once the butter has melted add the onion. Sauté for 3–5 minutes or until the onions are translucent and cooked through but not brown, and then add in the roasted garlic and butternut squash. Season well with salt and pepper. Cover and sweat for about 5 minutes. At this stage you can add the curry powder and curry paste, if you would like your soup to have a bit more kick.

In the meantime, heat the stock in another large saucepan. When it starts to simmer, add the roasted, spiced vegetable mix and, using a hand blender, blend to a smooth soup. Pour in the cream to give a silky finish.

To prepare the spices, dry fry the cumin, coriander and peppercorns in a small pan until they release their aroma. Then transfer to a pestle and mortar and grind roughly.

Place the butter and cinnamon stick in a small saucepan over a medium heat and when the butter begins to foam, add the mustard seeds. When they start popping, add the ground spices and mix well to combine. Remove from the heat and discard the cinnamon stick.

Serve the soup in warmed bowls and drizzle the buttery spice mixture over the top. Have an extra drizzle of cream if you like.

CHEF'S TIP

✦ Roasting the butternut squash in advance really improves the flavour and reduces the cooking time for the soup.

RUTH WASSEL'S MINESTRONE SOUP

✦✦✦

Not only did my friend and fellow chef Ruth mentor me in the early years but she also taught me so much about cooking and combining different flavours. There is no doubt that she was a great inspiration to me. She also introduced me to Italian cooking, which is her passion, as she lived in Italy for 10 years. As Ruth says, "A good store cupboard cannot be without tinned tomatoes and quality olive oil." This soup is so versatile that really anything goes, and it's a great way to use up broken bits of pasta left at the bottom of the packet.

prep: 20 minutes ✦ **cook**: 45 minutes ✦ **serves**: 8–10

100g streaky bacon

5 tbsp olive oil

2 onions, finely diced

2 carrots, finely diced

2 sticks of celery, finely diced

2 leeks, finely diced

1 tbsp chopped fresh sage

salt and freshly cracked black pepper

2 potatoes, peeled and finely diced

350g courgettes, finely diced

2 x 400g tins chopped tomatoes

1.7 litres chicken stock

2 x 400g tins haricot or cannellini beans, drained and rinsed

100g broken or small pasta pieces

1 tsp sugar, or more to taste

TO SERVE

white crusty bread

pesto or fresh basil (optional)

Parmesan cheese, shaved

Slice the bacon into strips. In a large saucepan, heat the oil and cook the bacon until golden. Reduce the heat and add in the onions, carrots, celery, leeks, sage, salt and pepper. Cover with a lid and allow to sweat until soft but not coloured. Then add the potatoes, courgettes, tomatoes and stock. Bring to a boil and reduce to simmer, with the lid on, for about 30 minutes. Then add the drained and rinsed beans and the pasta.

Cook for about 15 minutes or until the pasta is cooked. Taste, adjust the seasoning and if needed add a teaspoon of sugar, as it enhances the sweetness of the tinned tomatoes. Serve with crusty bread and garnish with Parmesan cheese and a drizzle of pesto or some fresh chopped basil leaves.

✦✦✦

CHEF'S TIP

✦ With this soup, you can leave things out or add things in depending on what's in your fridge. Feel free to experiment. Ruth likes to add a bag of baby spinach leaves and spice this up with some chilli flakes. She also loves to substitute diced chorizo for the bacon.

PORK RISSOLES WITH CUCUMBER RELISH

❖❖❖

These are essentially meatballs with a twist. Rissoles are traditionally breaded pastries filled with minced meat or fish and a béchamel sauce, then deep-fried. This is my interpretation of spicy rissoles and these ones are incredibly moreish.

prep: 15 minutes ✦ **chill**: 1 hour ✦ **cook**: 20 minutes ✦ **serves**: 6–10

FOR THE RISSOLES

50ml sunflower oil

1 red onion, peeled and finely diced

2 garlic cloves, finely chopped

3cm fresh ginger, peeled and grated

1 stalk of lemongrass, bruised, peeled and
    finely chopped

500g pork mince

100g pork, chicken or lamb's liver
    (optional)

1 free-range egg, lightly beaten

handful fresh coriander (stalks and leaves),
    finely chopped

1 tbsp oyster sauce

handful fresh breadcrumbs

½ tsp salt and freshly cracked black pepper

FOR THE CUCUMBER RELISH

2 cucumbers, peeled

250ml rice vinegar

150g sugar

2 tbsp boiling water

6 shallots, peeled and finely diced

2 tbsp finely chopped fresh root ginger

2 garlic cloves, finely chopped

2 bird's-eye chilli, finely chopped

pinch of salt

To make the rissoles, add 30ml oil to a pan over a medium heat and sauté the onions, garlic, ginger and lemongrass for about 5 minutes, until they are softened but not brown. Set aside to cool.

Once cool, put the onion mix into a large mixing bowl and add in the mince, liver, egg, coriander, oyster sauce and breadcrumbs. Season and mix well to combine. With clean hands, roll the mixture into balls about the size of golf balls (you should get around 16), and then flatten each one slightly.

Place the rissoles on a plate. Cover and refrigerate for 1 hour.

Meanwhile make the cucumber relish. Slice the cucumber very finely in long strips, ideally on a box grater or with a vegetable peeler, and then transfer to a medium-sized serving bowl. Combine the rice vinegar, sugar and water in a small pot and bring to the boil, stirring until the sugar has dissolved. Then add the shallots, ginger, garlic, chilli and salt. Allow to cool. Then pour the cooled dressing over the cucumber.

Preheat the oven to 160°C fan/180°C/gas mark 4.

In a shallow frying pan, heat the remaining 20ml of sunflower oil and fry the rissoles over a medium-high heat until lightly browned on both sides. You may need to do this in two batches.

Then transfer the rissoles to a baking sheet and cook for 10–15 minutes in the preheated oven.

Serve with the cucumber relish or tzatziki (see page 128).

CHEF'S TIP

✦ Fry off a small amount of the rissole mixture and taste before
    you finish seasoning.

COQ AU VIN

❖❖❖

The word "coq" in French means "rooster" or "cock", a tough bird that benefits hugely from braising. Traditionally this recipe needs more cooking time, but nowadays it's a relatively quick dish to prepare as birds are reared more quickly and are more tender. It's a delicious dish with incredible flavour.

prep: 30 minutes ✦ **marinate**: 24 hours ✦ **cook**: 1½ hours ✦ **serves**: 4

8 joints free-range chicken, to include thigh, leg and drumstick, on the bone

FOR THE MARINADE

750ml (1 bottle) good red wine (typically a Burgundy)

2 carrots, peeled and sliced into batons

2 celery stalks, peeled and sliced into batons

5 garlic cloves, peeled but left whole

1 tbsp peppercorns

150g shallots or baby onions, peeled but left whole

2 tbsp balsamic vinegar

bouquet garni, to include 2 bay leaves, parsley stalks, 6 sprigs thyme, 1 sprig rosemary

FOR THE CASSEROLE

a little sunflower oil, for frying

1 tbsp plain flour

75g butter

sprig of fresh thyme

500ml chicken stock

150g streaky bacon, chopped

350g button mushrooms, cleaned and cut in half

salt and freshly cracked black pepper

TO SERVE

creamy mash (see recipe on page 98)

handful of fresh parsley, chopped

green salad (optional)

To marinate the chicken, heat a heavy casserole pot and bring the wine to the boil and reduce by one-third. This will remove the alcohol and concentrate the colour and flavour. Leave to cool. In a bowl, mix the chicken pieces, carrot, celery, garlic, peppercorns, shallots/baby onions, balsamic vinegar and bouquet garni and pour the cooled red wine over them. Cover and refrigerate for 24 hours.

To cook the chicken, drain the chicken pieces and vegetables but reserve the liquid. Pat the chicken pieces dry with kitchen paper and season with salt and pepper. On a high heat, add vegetable oil to a large casserole pot. Brown the chicken pieces for 5 minutes on each side, skin side first. Transfer the browned chicken pieces to a plate.

Preheat the oven to 200°C fan/220°C/gas mark 4.

Place 1 tablespoon of flour in a small dish and toast it in the hot oven for 10 minutes. Remove and reduce oven to 160°C fan/180°C/gas 4.

Clean and dry the casserole pot. Place it over a medium heat and melt the butter. Add the marinated vegetables and fresh thyme. Cook gently until just browned. Spoon out any excess butter, add the toasted flour and stir gently. Slowly add the reserved marinade liquid, little by little. Add the stock as well. Cook gently over a low heat. Add the chicken pieces and return to the boil. Cover and transfer to the oven for 30 minutes.

Over a medium heat, fry the chopped bacon and button mushrooms. Add to the casserole when it has come out of the oven. Taste and correct the seasoning, if needed.

Serve with a dressed green salad and lashings of creamy mash.

CANNELLONI

❖❖❖

The first time I ate this dish was in Verona, Italy, while travelling around Europe in 1991. I remember it well because as I was sitting in a restaurant on Piazza Bra, tucking in to my cannelloni, I looked up to see the actors John Thaw and Kevin Whately walking past. They were followed by some cameramen and other crew — it turned out that they were shooting an Inspector Morse episode around Vicenza and Verona, "The Death of Self". I spent the rest of the day watching them filming — a great memory. This is a very rustic dish, so don't expect it to look like a da Vinci masterpiece!

prep: 20 minutes ✦ **cook**: 50 minutes ✦ **serves**: 4 as a main or 8 as a starter

FOR THE SAUCE

1 tbsp olive oil

2 garlic cloves, finely chopped

3 onions, finely chopped

2 x 400g tins chopped tomatoes

100ml red wine

500ml vegetable stock

handful of fresh basil (30g bag), chopped

1 tsp sugar

salt and freshly cracked black pepper

FOR THE FILLING

1 tbsp olive oil

175g beef mince

175g pork mince

1 tsp freshly ground nutmeg

1 tsp ground mace

1 tsp celery salt

1 tsp garlic salt

1 onion, sautéed (from above)

1 tsp salt and 1 tsp freshly cracked black
  pepper

FOR THE TOPPING

100g Parmesan cheese, grated

16 dried cannelloni pasta tubes (available
  from most good delis and supermarkets)

YOU WILL ALSO NEED

1 lasagne dish (30cm x 20cm)

To make the sauce, sauté the 3 onions and garlic in the oil in a large pan until the onions are translucent. Remove one-third of the sautéed onion mix and set it aside to add to the filling recipe later. Add the tomatoes to the remaining onion in the pan and cook for 5 minutes over a medium heat. Add the red wine and stock. Continue to cook over a high heat for 2 minutes. Then reduce the heat and simmer for 5 minutes, stirring occasionally. Add the chopped basil and season with salt and pepper. Remove from the heat and blend in a food processor (or with a hand blender) to make a lovely smooth sauce.

To make the filling, mix the minced meats together with a fork to combine. Heat the oil in the largest heavy-based pan you have and add in the mince. Season with a generous pinch of salt and pepper and add the remaining spices. Cook for 5–7 minutes, turning the meat several times, until it is completely browned. Add the sautéed onion and 3 tablespoons of the tomato sauce mixture, and stir to combine.

Preheat the oven to 160°C fan/180°C/gas mark 4.

To assemble the cannelloni, lightly butter a lasagne dish. Using a piping bag or a teaspoon, fill each tube with 1–2 tablespoons of minced-meat filling. Line up the cannelloni side by side, nice and tight, in the dish.

Reheat the tomato sauce and spoon it over the cannelloni to cover them completely. Sprinkle the Parmesan cheese over the top and cover with a lid or tinfoil. Bake in the preheated oven for 40 minutes. Remove the lid or tin foil 10–15 minutes before the end of the cooking time to allow the top to brown.

MOUSSAKA

◆◆◆

This traditional aubergine-based dish is popular in Balkan and Mediterranean cuisines and there are many local and regional variations. The dish, in its various guises, is found throughout the countries of the former Ottoman Empire. In Greece it is typically a layered dish and is enjoyed hot, but it's lovely served cold as well. The top layer of this dish has the most beautiful soft and creamy texture, not unlike a panna cotta. You can replace the aubergine with courgette if you like.

prep: 1½ hours ◆ **cook**: 1 hour ◆ **serves**: 8

2 large aubergines (about 275g each), trimmed and sliced about ½ cm thick

2 tsp rock salt

sunflower or vegetable oil, for frying

2 onions, finely diced

4 garlic cloves, finely chopped

750g minced beef or lamb

salt and freshly cracked black pepper

200ml red wine

2 tsp allspice

1½ tsp ground cinnamon

1 tbsp dried oregano

1 tsp grated nutmeg

3 bay leaves

1 tbsp sugar

1 tsp celery salt or celery seeds

1 litre beef stock

2 x 400g tins chopped tomatoes

FOR THE BÉCHAMEL (WHITE) SAUCE

80g butter

80g plain flour

800ml milk

salt and freshly cracked black pepper

2 tbsp chopped fresh parsley

250g Parmesan, grated

100ml cream

4 free-range egg yolks, lightly beaten

Preheat the oven to 200°C fan/220°C/gas mark 7. Place the aubergine slices in a colander and sprinkle with rock salt. Let them sit until you can see the liquid coming to the surface, about 20–30 minutes. Rinse the slices well and pat them dry. Roast in the hot oven for 18 minutes. Remove from the oven and allow to cool. Alternatively you can fry the aubergine on both sides in a frying pan with a little olive oil. Remove and drain on kitchen paper.

In a large saucepan gently sauté the onion and garlic in a little oil for 3–5 minutes or until softened. Season with salt and pepper. Remove from the heat. In a separate saucepan or frying pan, brown the beef (or lamb) in small batches. When the beef is browned, add it to the onions and garlic in the large saucepan. Deglaze the pan (see chef's tip) used to cook the meat with 2 tbsp of red wine and pour the liquid into the large saucepan. Add the allspice, cinnamon, oregano, nutmeg, bay leaves, sugar and celery salt. Season again with salt and pepper, if required. Add the remaining wine, the stock and the tomatoes. Increase the heat for 5 minutes until the mixture reaches boiling point. Reduce the heat and simmer for 60 minutes. Remove from heat. Allow to cool. Skim off any excess fat.

To make the white sauce, place a medium saucepan over a medium heat. Melt the butter and then add the flour and stir until the butter and flour are well combined. Pour in the milk gradually, whisking constantly as the mixture thickens. Add more milk until the consistency is nice and thick. Season with salt and pepper. Add the chopped parsley. Simmer for 5 minutes. Remove from the heat and stir in the Parmesan and cream. Allow to cool completely. Whisk in the egg yolks and fold in the beaten egg whites.

Preheat the oven to 160°C fan/180°C/gas mark 4.

Continued overleaf

2 free-range egg whites, beaten to stiff
  peaks

200g white breadcrumbs (made from
  approx 7 slices of bread)

50g Parmesan, grated

1 rectangular baking dish (about 25cm x
  25cm x 7cm)

While the béchamel mixture is cooling, prepare the baking dish for the moussaka by greasing it with a little butter and then sprinkling half the breadcrumbs over the base of the baking dish. Cover with half the mince mixture, followed by a layer of aubergine slices, then a layer of béchamel. Repeat with another layer of breadcrumbs, mince mixture, aubergine and béchamel. Sprinkle the top with Parmesan. Cover with tin foil.

Bake in the oven for 60 minutes. Remove from the oven and allow to settle for 10 minutes before serving.

CHEF'S TIPS

+ To deglaze means to loosen and dissolve the brown residue left at the bottom of a pan in order to release the flavour for a gravy or a sauce.

+ This is a great dish to cook a day in advance and then reheat for 30 minutes in an oven preheated to 150°C fan/170°C/gas mark 3 or until warmed through.

+ Sprinkling salt over aubergine slices before cooking draws out the vegetable's moisture and is known as "degorging". It really improves the flavour of the cooked aubergine.

+ Instead of roasting the aubergine you can grill them on a hot griddle pan for 3 minutes each side.

+ Remove any grease or fat from the surface of the cooked mince. There could be up to 150ml, depending on the fat content of the mince.

IAN GAMBLE'S MOROCCAN LAMB AND APRICOT FAJITAS

❖❖❖

The Tex-Mex term "fajita" commonly refers to any grilled meat served as a taco on a flour or corn tortilla. Fajitas as we know them today — with the Spanish nickname, the cheap cut of meat and cooked on a campfire or a grill — date from the 1930s and originated on the ranch lands of south and west Texas. During cattle round-ups, animals were butchered regularly to feed the cowhands. Throwaway cuts like the hide, the head and the entrails, and trimmings such as skirt, were given to the Mexican cowboys, called vaqueros, *as part of their pay. My friend Ian Gamble kindly gave me this recipe. I'm not sure if he thinks of himself as the cowboy or the cattle rancher but I know this is a really tasty dish that's great to share with friends.*

prep: 20 minutes ✦ **cook**: 30 minutes ✦ **serves**: 5

500g lamb mince

2 tbsp olive oil

1 large onion, chopped

1 garlic clove, chopped

½ tsp ground cumin

½ tsp ground cinnamon

½ tsp ground coriander

1 tsp chilli powder

3 medium-sized carrots, peeled and grated

2 tbsp tomato purée

150g chopped dried apricots

500ml chicken stock

3 tbsp crème fraîche

juice of 1 lime

handful chopped fresh parsley

TO SERVE

handful cherry tomatoes, chopped

100g grated mozzarella cheese

5 large tortilla wraps

Place a large pan over a medium heat, add a little oil and fry off the mince until browned. Then remove the mince from the pan and set aside, draining off any excess oil or fat. Add 2 tablespoons of olive oil to the pan and over a low heat cook the chopped onion and garlic until soft. Add the spices — cumin, cinnamon, coriander and chilli — and cook for a further 2–3 minutes. Add more chilli if you want to spice things up. Then add in the grated carrots and cook for another minute.

Now add the mince back into the pan, followed by the tomato purée, the chopped apricots and the chicken stock.

Mix gently and bring to a simmer in the pan. Cover and cook for about 20–30 minutes until all the juices have been absorbed into the meat. Mix through the crème fraîche. Add the lime juice and stir well. Sprinkle over the chopped parsley.

Warm the tortilla breads for about 20 seconds in a dry pan over a medium heat, just before serving. Serve the chilli with the mozzarella cheese and chopped cherry tomatoes sprinkled over and let your guests help themselves.

CHEF'S TIP

✦ This is delicious served up with my homemade guacamole (see recipe on page 151) and tomato salsa (see recipe on page 80).

CHILLI CON CARNE

❖

This is one of my favourite dishes — it's comfort food at its best. I have been making chilli for years and have tried many different variations. But I always come back to this recipe as it combines so many different elements. In fact, for years chilli was the only thing I'd make when I had friends around for supper. My friend JP still always asks, "What's for dinner? Chilli?" This one's for you, JP.

prep: 10 minutes ✦ **cook**: 45 minutes ✦ **serves**: 8

1 tbsp olive oil

1 medium onion, finely chopped

3 garlic cloves, crushed

2 stalks of celery, peeled and roughly chopped, including the leaves

1 red chilli (including seeds), chopped

1 green chilli (including seeds), chopped

100g chorizo sausage, cut into small cubes

5 back rashers, cut into strips

1kg lean minced beef

1 tbsp balsamic vinegar

120ml red wine

1 level tsp ground mace

2 level tsp chilli powder

2 level tsp ground cumin

1 level tsp cayenne pepper

1 tbsp dried or chopped fresh oregano

1 x 400g tin chopped tomatoes

2 tsp brown sugar

1 tbsp tomato paste

1 x 400g tin kidney beans, drained and rinsed

500ml beef stock

2 tsp salt and ½ tsp pepper

TO SERVE

steamed rice

grated cheese

sour cream or crème fraîche

Heat the olive oil in the largest heavy-based pan you have and add the chopped onion, garlic, celery, chilli, chorizo and bacon. Season with pepper and 2 teaspoons salt. Sauté over a medium heat for 5 minutes, stirring occasionally.

Transfer the contents of the pan to a large bowl or Pyrex dish, and then fry off the minced beef in small batches in the same pan. Cook for 5–7 minutes, turning the meat several times, until it is completely browned. Remove from the heat and add the cooked mince into the bowl and mix to combine all the cooked ingredients.

Deglaze (see chef's tip) the pan with the balsamic vinegar and red wine. This will pick up all that lovely meaty flavour that's been left at the bottom of the pan. Return all the cooked ingredients to the pan, stir and place over a medium heat. Add the mace, chilli powder, cumin, cayenne pepper and oregano and stir well. Cook for 2 minutes. Add the chopped tomatoes, sugar, tomato paste, kidney beans and beef stock. Stir to combine and simmer gently over a low heat for 30 minutes, uncovered. Season again with salt and pepper, if desired.

Serve in warmed bowls with fluffy, steamed rice, grated cheese and a dollop of sour cream or crème fraîche.

———— ❖ ————

CHEF'S TIPS

✦ To get the best flavour, prepare this dish a day in advance. It's also a good idea to remove any surplus grease or fat from the cooked chilli. You can store this in the fridge for a few days and simply reheat it gently on the hob. You can also freeze whatever you don't eat.

✦ To deglaze means to loosen and dissolve the brown residue left at the bottom of a pan in order to release the flavour for a gravy or a sauce.

ALMOND AND LEMON MERINGUES

When we were devising a new Spanish menu for Medley, Paul and I looked through a lot of cookbooks for inspiration. A recipe that particularly excited us was one for Spanish toasted-almond and lemon meringues in Rick Stein's Spain *cookbook. This is our interpretation of that recipe. I met Rick in Dublin last year when he was promoting his new book. He is an absolute gentleman and an inspiration to anyone who cooks; he's certainly my food hero.*

prep: 15 minutes ✦ **cook**: 1 hour ✦ **serves**: 4

100g flaked almonds

3 medium free-range egg whites

110g caster sugar or 125g icing sugar

zest of 1 lemon

TO SERVE

300 ml softly whipped cream or ice cream (optional)

200g fresh fruit (optional)

Preheat the oven to 200°C fan/220°C/gas mark 7.

Line two baking trays with parchment paper. On one tray spread the almonds over the parchment paper in an even layer and bake for 7 minutes or until golden brown.

Reduce the oven temperature to 130°C fan/150°C/gas mark 2.

In a clean, dry bowl whisk the egg whites until they form soft peaks. Gradually add the sugar and lemon zest, and whisk until the mixture forms stiff peaks.

Fold in the toasted almonds using a metal spoon.

Using a dessertspoon, dollop 24 egg-sized amounts of the meringue mixture onto the second lined baking tray, leaving a gap between each one, as they will expand during cooking. Place the tray in the oven and bake at 130°C fan/150°C/gas mark 2 for 60 minutes until slightly golden. Then turn the oven off. Leave them in the cooling oven to crisp up for about an hour.

Serve while still warm and sticky, with coffee, or leave to cool on a rack and serve with decadent dollops of softly whipped cream and fresh fruit. You can also sandwich two meringues together with a layer of cream and fresh fruit of your choice.

Store leftover meringues in an airtight container. They will stay fresh for up to 1 week.

CHOCOLATE BROWNIES

Brownies are a cross between a cookie and a cake. They usually have one of two different textures — fudge or cake. The fudgy brownie should be moist and dense, while the cake brownie is normally light and airy. This recipe is a cross pollination of the two textures. I have to admit that I think it's divine.

prep: 20 minutes ✦ **cook**: 35 minutes ✦ **makes**: 16 slices

100g pistachio nuts, shelled

100g butter, cut into cubes

130g dark chocolate (70 per cent cocoa solids), broken into pieces

2 free-range eggs, separated

225g caster sugar

100g plain flour, sifted

½ tbsp vanilla extract

zest of ½ orange

YOU WILL ALSO NEED

20cm square baking tin

Preheat the oven to 180°C fan/200°C/gas mark 6. Grease the baking tin with a little butter or a brush of vegetable oil.

Spread the pistachio nuts over a baking tray and toast them in the oven for 10 minutes. Remove and allow to cool. Gently crush the nuts using a pestle and mortar, or roughly chop.

Place a heatproof bowl over a shallow pan of gently simmering water (to make a bain-marie). Add the butter and chocolate to the bowl and allow them to melt slowly.

In a bowl whisk the egg yolks to a nice creamy texture, and in a separate dry, clean bowl whisk the egg whites until they form stiff peaks.

Combine the sugar and flour in a mixing bowl. Then add the melted chocolate-and-butter mixture, followed by the egg yolks, vanilla extract, orange zest and half of the crushed toasted pistachio nuts. Mix well to combine. Finally, fold in the egg whites. Transfer the mixture to a lined and greased baking tin and bake in the preheated oven for 35 minutes. When cooked, the brownies should be crisp on top and soft on the inside.

Allow to cool and then slice. Garnish with the remaining pistachio nuts.

CHEF'S TIP

✦ You can double up the recipe and use a larger baking tray. I tend to do this for larger parties. They will keep in an airtight container for up to 3 days, staying lovely and moist, or you can freeze them.

ROZANNA PURCELL'S GUILT-FREE BANOFFEE

Banoffee is traditionally a pie made with a biscuit or pastry base, topped with toffee, cream and banana — the toffee is made from boiled condensed milk. Here, model Roz Purcell shares her dairy-free, low-calorie version, which is much lighter in saturated fat than a traditional banoffee, but wait until you taste it! Her combination of flavours works amazingly well. Roz likes to use the American cup system for measuring, which makes the recipe so simple to follow and replicate.

prep: 25 minutes ✦ **serves**: 6

FOR THE BASE

1 cup dates, pitted

2 cups walnuts

pinch of sea salt

FOR THE CARAMEL LAYER

2 cups dates, pitted

½ cup coconut water

pinch of sea salt

2 tsp vanilla extract

FOR THE BANANA MOUSSE

3-4 tbsp tahini

3 ripe bananas, peeled and mashed

4 tbsp coconut butter

2 tbsp coconut water

2 tsp vanilla extract

1 tbsp freshly squeezed lemon juice

FOR THE CREAM FROSTING

1 x tin of coconut milk, refrigerated

TO GARNISH

banana chips (optional)

cocoa powder (optional)

YOU WILL ALSO NEED

6 small jam jars or small kilner jars

To make the base, place all the base ingredients in a food processor and blend until the mixture is fine and comes together. Divide the base mixture equally between the 6 jam jars and press down with the back of a spoon. Place the jars in the fridge while you prepare the next layer.

To make the caramel layer, place all the caramel ingredients in the food processor and blend until they form a smooth, thick caramel with no lumps. Pour this caramel mixture over the base, dividing it equally between the 6 jars.

To make the mousse, simply place all the mousse ingredients in the food processor and blend until creamy. Then spoon the mixture on top of the caramel layer, dividing it equally between the 6 jars.

To finish, open the can of refrigerated coconut milk and scoop out the hardened milk that will have formed on the top. Spread a little of this over the top of each banoffee and then sprinkle with cocoa powder and banana chips if you like.

FRIENDS FOR SUPPER

BELLA ITALIA

Mozzarella and Parma ham with a chilli, garlic and olive dressing
Cannelloni
Almond and lemon meringues

Wine suggestions
White: a full-bodied, crisp Lugana ✦ Red: a robust Montepulciano d'Abruzzo

SPIRIT WARMING

Pork rissoles with cucumber relish
Coq au vin
Rozanna Purcell's guilt-free banoffee

Wine suggestions
Red: a soft, ripe Burgundy Pinot noir or a good quality Chianti Classico

HOME COMFORT

Ruth Wassel's minestrone soup
Moussaka
Chocolate brownies

Wine suggestions
White: an elegant Italian Soave ✦ Red: a big, rich Cabernet from Lebanon

ELEGANT
DINNER PARTY

◆◆◆

This chapter is for when you want to go the extra mile — perhaps you're thinking of throwing a New Year's Eve party for 10–12 people or inviting close friends and family around to celebrate a special birthday. Whatever the occasion, the recipes here will inspire and impress. The dishes are a little bit more involved, but there are always elements that can be made a day or two in advance so you don't get stressed on the day itself. For this kind of evening I would recommend serving some lovely light bites or canapés when your guests arrive, to set the mood. Presentation is key here. It doesn't take much to lift the dishes, so try to use some imagination when plating up. All it takes is a simple garnish — think colour and art on the plate. Edible flowers, fresh herbs and the components of the dish can be used for presentation and will really add that final flourish the occasion deserves.

CRAB AND APPLE BITES

This is great as a light canapé. It also works well as a starter, served with baby salad leaves. Try to use sweet brown and white meat. The crab mixture in this recipe has great texture and beautiful flavour with a slight kick from the Tabasco.

prep: 5 minutes ✦ **serves**: 7 starter portions or 50 canapés (on spoons)

1 green eating apple (Granny Smith), peeled, cored and finely chopped or coarsely grated

juice of 1 lemon, strained

500g crab meat, drained

2 tbsp mayonnaise

salt and freshly cracked black pepper

½ tsp Tabasco (optional)

TO SERVE

1 tbsp chopped fresh flat-leaf parsley

1 tbsp chopped fresh coriander (optional)

YOU WILL ALSO NEED

Chinese spoons or dessertspoons, to present

Pour half of the lemon juice over the chopped (or grated) apple to prevent it from discolouring while you prepare the crab.

Flake the crab meat into a bowl with a fork. Stir in the mayonnaise. Season with salt, pepper and Tabasco (if you want to add a bit of kick). Add the chopped apple and stir in the remaining lemon juice. Taste and season as needed, adding more salt, pepper or Tabasco, to taste.

Divide the mixture between the number of spoons you're using and garnish each one with chopped parsley and coriander (if using).

CHEF'S TIP

✦ If serving this as a canapé, allow for 3 canapés each and 10g per spoon. This recipe makes enough canapés for a dinner party of 16 guests. Alternatively you will get 7 starter portions by using a 6cm x 3cm circular pastry cutter as a mould, allowing 70g per portion

ROPE-GROWN MUSSELS WITH A TOMATO SALSA

Last year Medley hosted the launch party for the Westport Festival of Music and Food and we got 10kg of fresh mussels delivered from Killary Harbour in the West of Ireland, where they've been farming mussels since the 1980s. As a natural fjord — it's 15km long, 0.7km wide and 15m deep — it is ideal for growing rope mussels. To reflect the quality of this wonderful natural Irish ingredient, we wanted to create a dish that would excite the palate. What we came up with is a canapé bursting with flavour and vitality. You'll find them photographed on page 79.

prep: 10 minutes ✦ **cook**: 10 minutes ✦ **serves**: up to 10

FOR THE MUSSELS

1kg mussels

1 tbsp olive oil

5 whole garlic cloves, peeled

150ml white wine

FOR THE SALSA

2 large vine-ripened tomatoes, peeled and finely chopped

1 tbsp red wine vinegar

4 tbsp extra virgin olive oil

1 tbsp capers, finely chopped

1 small red onion, finely chopped

1 red pepper, deseeded and finely chopped

1 green pepper, deseeded and finely chopped

3 garlic cloves, finely chopped

1 tbsp chopped fresh flat leaf parsley

salt and freshly cracked black pepper, to taste

Wash the mussels in cold water. Scrub off any rough barnacles and pull off the beard. Discard any chipped or open mussels. Soak in clean, cold water for 20 minutes and then drain.

In a large saucepan heat the olive oil with the whole cloves of garlic. Add the mussels and white wine. Shake, cover and cook over a high heat for approximately 5 minutes or until the shells have all opened. Remove from the heat, drain and allow to cool for 10 minutes. Discard any mussels that have failed to open. Remove the top shell from each mussel and discard. Then loosen the mussel from its base shell so that it is just sitting in the shell. Now arrange them on a serving platter.

Make the salsa by putting all the ingredients in a bowl and mixing well. Taste for seasoning. If you want a smooth texture, blend in a food processor, but you can serve it just as it is.

To serve, spoon 2 teaspoons of the tomato salsa over each mussel and serve immediately. Alternatively serve 6 mussels per person, out of the shell on a small serving platter drizzled with the salsa.

CHEF'S TIP

✦ You may want to place paper napkins under the mussels so they don't slide all over the serving platter.

1kg

Cat II   FRANCE
Tomate Variété
Ana...

1kg

Cat II   FRANCE
Tomate Variété
Cœur de Bœuf

ARANCINI RISOTTO BALLS WITH WILD MUSHROOMS

◆◆◆

I was recently doing an Italian cookery demonstration and I introduced this lovely "Italian" recipe to my guests. One of them was very quick to correct me, saying rather forcefully that this recipe was not Italian. I was quite embarrassed. It turned out that she was from Palermo in Sicily and so is this recipe. Oops! You can skip the rolling stage of this recipe and simply serve it as risotto, to serve 8 as a starter or 4 as a main course.

prep: 25 minutes ◆ **cook**: 45 minutes ◆ **makes**: up to 35 large or 70 small balls

FOR THE RISOTTO

15g dried mushrooms, porcini or similar

120g butter

400g Arborio risotto rice

200ml white wine

1 litre vegetable stock (or chicken, if preferred)

1 onion (approx 150g), finely diced

2 tbsp finely chopped fresh thyme

80g Parmesan or white Cheddar cheese (or a mix is great)

salt and freshly cracked black pepper

OPTIONAL

¼ tsp saffron

150g peas, cooked

FOR THE RISOTTO BALL COATING

150g plain flour

2 eggs, lightly beaten

250g breadcrumbs

2 litres vegetable or sunflower oil, for deep-frying

Place the dried (porcini) mushrooms in a small bowl and just cover with 250ml of boiling water. Let them soak and soften for 15 minutes. Remove from the liquid, squeeze out the excess water and finely chop the mushrooms. Retain the liquid, as this lovely mushroom-flavoured stock is wonderful added in when you are cooking the rice.

To make the risotto, melt 40g butter in a large heavy-based pan over a medium heat. Add the risotto rice and mix well to ensure that all the rice grains are coated with butter. Add the wine and stir until it has been absorbed by the rice. Add 100ml of the vegetable stock and stir gently. Once the vegetable stock has been absorbed, add 100ml of the mushroom stock. Continue adding the stocks like this until all of them have been absorbed and the rice is almost cooked. Add the saffron (if using). This will take 20–25 minutes. Remove from the heat. Add 60g of butter and stir well. You can serve the risotto just like this if you like.

In a separate pan, add the remaining 20g butter and sauté the onion, thyme and mushrooms over a medium heat for 5 minutes. Season with salt and pepper. Then add the onion mixture into the risotto and stir well. Place the risotto back over a medium heat and continue cooking until the rice is fully cooked (about 5 minutes). Stir in the cheese and season with salt and pepper, as desired. Finally, add the cooked peas, if using. Remove from heat and leave to cool completely. Overnight is ideal.

Continued overleaf

To make small risotto balls, gather an amount of cold risotto roughly the size of a table-tennis ball and work it into a ball using the palms of your hands. Go for a golf-ball-sized amount to make larger arancini. Then dip in flour, then egg, then breadcrumbs. Place on a tray or plate and transfer to the fridge to firm up for 30 minutes.

Heat the oil in a large saucepan over a medium heat. (Alternatively you can use a deep fat fryer heated to 180°C). Deep-fry the balls, in batches, for 5 to 6 minutes or until golden brown. Transfer to kitchen paper to absorb any excess oil.

Serve the arancini immediately.

CHEF'S TIPS

+ If you absolutely must cook them significantly in advance of serving, place the arancini in a 140°C fan/160°C/gas 3 oven for 15–20 minutes before serving.

+ *Arancini* or *arancine* are fried rice balls coated with breadcrumbs, said to have originated in Sicily in the tenth century. The name derives from the food's shape and colour, which is reminiscent of an orange (the Italian word for orange is *arancia*, and *arancina* means "little orange").

FILLET OF BEEF WITH HORSERADISH

＊＊＊

This is one of the most popular canapés we serve in Medley and at weddings or private parties. The method of cooking the beef is exactly the same as the fillet of beef recipe on page 32. I recommend cooking the beef rare, as it looks much better on the plate. The beef for this canapé is best cooked a day in advance as the dish is served cold. Any leftover beef can be served on a cold meat platter for a lovely long, lazy lunch. I love presenting it with some freshly grated horseradish.

prep: 10 minutes ✦ **chill**: 2 hours or overnight ✦ **cook**: 20-50 minutes ✦ **makes**: up to 50

FOR THE BEEF
500g beef fillet, well trimmed

50ml olive oil

FOR THE HORSERADISH SAUCE
1 x 200g tub crème fraîche

2 tbsp horseradish sauce

2 tsp freshly grated horseradish (optional)

TO SERVE
Chinese spoons

fresh chives

To prepare the beef, trim the fillet to remove any sinew, outer layers of fat or white membrane.

Tightly wrap the fillet in cling film and then in tin foil. Place in the fridge overnight or for a minimum of 2 hours. Make sure to remove the beef from the fridge at least one hour before you are going to cook it, to allow it to come back up to room temperature.

Preheat the oven to 200°C fan/220°C/gas mark 7.

To cook the beef, heat a large non-stick frying pan over a medium-high heat and add the olive oil. When the pan is very hot, add the beef and sear it on all sides for 1½–2 minutes on each side until evenly browned all over. Then transfer to a roasting tin.

Place the roasting tin in the oven for 12 minutes for rare beef, 20 minutes for medium rare, 30 minutes for medium, or 45 minutes for well done. Then remove the beef and allow to cool. Cover and place in the fridge overnight.

To make the horseradish sauce, combine all the ingredients in a mixing bowl and mix well.

To serve, slice the fillet of beef in half horizontally, creating 2 long pieces, and then slice the beef very thinly.

Use Chinese spoons or any large spoons of your choice, and layer the spoon with rocket and then a strip of beef. You can decide whether you prefer to roll the beef or present it flat. Then, using a teaspoon, top the beef with a small amount of horseradish sauce. You can also garnish with some fresh chives.

CHEF'S TIP
✦ This canapé must be served immediately, as the beef dries out very quickly. Assemble the components just before serving. You can also roll the beef strips, filled with a teaspoon of the horseradish sauce, and serve on a large platter.

CAULIFLOWER SOUP

◆◆◆

I was doing a dinner party for a client a number of years ago and he had a weak spot for cauliflower and a love of soup. So I thought, let's combine the two. I couldn't find any recipes for cauliflower soup that I liked, so I came up with this very simple creation. It has a beautiful velvety texture, with a taste to match.

prep: 10 minutes ◆ **cook**: 30 minutes ◆ **serves**: 10–12

80g butter

1 onion, finely chopped

2 garlic cloves, finely chopped

2 heads cauliflower, cut into florets (retain the green leaves and stalks)

salt and freshly cracked black pepper

2 litres chicken or vegetable stock

200ml milk

100ml cream, plus a little extra to serve

2 tsp freshly ground nutmeg

Melt 50g butter in a large heavy-bottomed pan over a medium heat. Sweat the onion and garlic with the green leaves and stalks of the cauliflower until all the ingredients become soft but still hold their shape. Season with salt and pepper. Add the cauliflower florets and then the stock. Cook until the cauliflower is soft. Add the milk and cream and bring almost up to the boil but be sure not to boil the liquid.

Season with nutmeg, taste, and add more salt and pepper if needed. Remove from the heat and liquidise using a hand blender.

Serve the soup in warmed bowls, with crusty bread, and garnish with a swirl of cream.

GARLIC CHILLI PRAWNS

This is a beautifully vibrant and tasty dish. It's quick, simple, aromatic and the prawns are wonderfully succulent. What more can I say to sell it? For this recipe you can shell, clean and devein the prawns or leave them whole.

prep: 5 minutes ✦ **cook**: 5 minutes ✦ **serves**: 4

450g large prawns

1 green bird's-eye chilli

1 red bird's-eye chilli

50g unsalted butter

4 garlic cloves, finely chopped

freshly cracked salt and pepper

TO SERVE

2 fresh limes, cut into quarters

crusty white bread (optional)

For this recipe you can remove the heads and shells of the prawns or leave them on – whichever way you prefer to serve them.

Finely chop the chillies. If you like spicy food, leave the seeds in; if you prefer milder food, remove the seeds.

Melt the butter in a heavy-based frying pan. Add the chillies and garlic and cook until softened (about 2 minutes). Do not let the garlic brown as this will make it taste bitter.

Add the prawns to the pan and cook for about 3 minutes, until they turn pink, turning them several times. Season with salt and pepper before serving.

Serve with wedges of fresh lime and some crusty white bread.

CHEF'S TIPS

✦ To remove the shell from a prawn, grip the body of the prawn in one hand and twist the head off with the other. Turn the prawn over and pull the shell open along the length of the belly, working from the head down, gently prising it open so that you can pull the prawn free. Once the shell is off, check to see if there is a black vein running down the back of the prawn. Using a small, sharp knife, make a shallow cut along the length of the black line and then lift it out using the tip of the knife.

✦ Leave a fingerbowl of warm water on the table with a lemon wedge in it for guests to clean their fingers after removing the shells from the prawns.

✦ You can also use raw frozen tiger prawns for this recipe.

SMOKED SALMON BLINIS

—— ✦✦✦ ——

I serve this canapé at almost all of my parties and functions. You can play around with the blini topping and with the way you serve the salmon — chopped, diced or simply rolled. If you really want to spoil or impress your guests, you could serve it with fish roe or caviar. I have given you the recipe for making your own blinis but you can of course buy them ready-made.

prep: 20 minutes ✦ **rest**: 2 hours ✦ **cook**: up to 10 minutes ✦ **makes**: 50 blinis

FOR THE BLINIS

175ml milk

150ml crème fraîche

50g buckwheat flour

115g strong white flour

½ tsp salt

7g caster sugar

7g sachet dried yeast

2 organic eggs, separated

25g butter

vegetable oil, for frying the blinis

FOR THE TOPPING

250g sliced smoked salmon

250ml crème fraîche

2 tbsp chopped fresh dill

1 tbsp freshly squeezed lemon juice

freshly cracked salt and pepper

TO SERVE

sprigs of fresh dill, optional

To make the blini batter, pour the milk into a small saucepan, add the crème fraîche and heat very gently (note that high heat will damage the yeast).

Sift the flours into a clean dry bowl. Add the salt and sugar. Sprinkle in the yeast.

Add the egg yolks and 25g butter to the milk. Whisk and pour over the flour mixture. Continue whisking until you have a thick batter. Cover and leave in a warm place for 1 hour. After 1 hour the batter will be soft, light, spongy and bubbly.

In the meantime, whisk the egg whites until they form stiff peaks. Gently fold into the batter. Cover again and allow to stand for a further 1 hour.

Heat a frying pan over a medium heat. Add a little vegetable oil and a small spoonful of batter to the pan (it should be about 4cm in diameter when it hits the pan). After 60 seconds, flip the blini and cook for a further 30 seconds on the reverse side or until golden brown on both sides. As with making pancakes, you need to season the pan, so be prepared to discard your first one or two blinis, but the rest will work perfectly once the pan has come up to the right temperature. Transfer cooked blinis to a wire rack and repeat until the batter is used up. When the blinis have cooled, wrap them in tin foil to make parcels (6 per parcel).

To make the salmon topping, mix the crème fraîche with the chopped dill and lemon juice and season lightly with salt and pepper.

To serve, reheat the blinis (in the tin-foil parcels) in a low oven (120°C fan/140°C/gas mark 1) for 8 minutes. Top each blini with thin slices of salmon, add the crème fraîche mixture and garnish with sprigs of fresh dill.

SUMMER SMOKED HADDOCK MOUSSE

———— ❖❖❖ ————

This is a recipe that brings me back to my childhood. It's adapted from the recipe of a great family friend, Joyce Whelehan. It reminds me of the wonderful summers I enjoyed in Offaly with my brothers and sisters and the multitude of foreign students who came to stay with us to learn English.

prep: 20 minutes ✦ **chill**: 24 hours ✦ **serves**: 8–10

8 gelatine sheets (or 8 tsp powdered
  gelatine)

150ml stock (chicken, vegetable or fish)

FOR THE POACHED HADDOCK

400g smoked haddock

500ml milk

1 tsp freshly grated nutmeg

3 bay leaves

FOR THE WHITE SAUCE

25g butter

25g plain flour

250ml poaching liquid from the haddock
  (or milk)

pinch freshly grated nutmeg

salt and freshly cracked black pepper

200ml mayonnaise

200ml whipped cream

2 tsp Tabasco sauce, or to taste

juice of ½ lemon

FOR THE VEGETABLES

2 large carrots, peeled and diced

2 green peppers, deseeded and diced

125g peas

1 small tin (about 160g) sweetcorn, drained

½ onion, grated

2 tomatoes, chopped

Place the haddock in a pan with the milk, nutmeg and bay leaves, and poach gently for about 8 minutes over a medium heat. Remove the fish with a slotted spoon and set aside to cool. Retain the poaching liquid as you will need it to make the white sauce. Remove all bones and skin from the haddock and break the fish into bite-size pieces.

To make the white sauce, set a small saucepan over a medium heat and melt the butter. Add the flour and stir until the butter and flour are well combined. Pour in the poaching liquid from the haddock (or milk), whisking continuously. As the sauce thickens add more liquid if needed. Season with a pinch of nutmeg and salt and pepper. Set aside.

Prepare the carrots, pepper and peas by cooking them for 5 minutes in a pot of lightly salted boiling water and then blanching them in ice-cold water to cool. Drain and set aside.

Mix the haddock, blanched vegetables, sweetcorn, grated onion and tomatoes in a bowl. Set aside.

Prepare the sheets of gelatine by soaking them in a bowl of cold water for 5 minutes, allowing them to swell slightly. Remove from the water and gently squeeze out any excess liquid. Place the gelatine in a small saucepan with 150ml of the stock. Gently heat until completely dissolved. Remove from the heat.

Add the gelatine mixture to the white sauce by straining it through a fine sieve. Then add mayonnaise and fold in the whipped cream. Add the Tabasco and lemon juice and season with salt and pepper. Taste and adjust seasoning as required.

To assemble the dish, use a fish mould or high-sided serving dish. Place the poached haddock in the mould and then add the mixed vegetables, followed by the hard-boiled eggs. Cover with the white sauce mixture, adding just enough to cover the

TO ASSEMBLE

4 hard-boiled eggs, quartered

2 tbsp chopped fresh parsley or chives

1 cucumber, thinly sliced

other ingredients — you don't want it to be too wet. Sprinkle over the fresh herbs. Cover and refrigerate until set. Garnish with overlapping slices of cucumber.

Serve chilled with baby new potatoes and salad.

CHICKEN LIVER PÂTÉ

❖❖❖

I first tried chicken liver pâté when I went on a school exchange to France in 1987. I have been making this for years, with a few tweaks and changes over time. It's a dish that always tantalises the taste buds.

prep: 15 minutes ✦ **cook**: 10 minutes ✦ **serves**: 8–10

750g butter, softened

1 large onion or 4 shallots, diced

2 large garlic cloves, crushed

2 tbsp chopped fresh thyme

1kg chicken liver, trimmed

salt and freshly cracked black pepper (about 2 tsp of each)

50ml Madeira, sweet sherry, Cognac or dessert wine

Place a large, heavy-bottomed pan over a medium heat and melt a large knob of butter. Sweat the onion (or shallots) with the garlic and thyme for about five minutes.

Add the chicken livers and sauté them until they are pink and almost cooked through. Season with salt and pepper. Add the Madeira (or the sherry or cognac). Cook on a high heat for 4 minutes to burn off the alcohol, and then remove from the heat.

Scrape the mixture carefully into a food processor and blend for a couple of minutes.

Hold back 125g butter and place it in a Pyrex jug and set aside. Add the remaining butter in to the food processor and whizz for 30–60 seconds until the mixture is nice and smooth. Pour the pâté mixture into a serving bowl and allow to cool at room temperature.

To make clarified butter, melt the reserved 125g of butter in a small saucepan over a medium heat. Remove from the heat and pour into a Pyrex jug. When the solids float to the surface, skim them off with a slotted spoon. The remainder of the milk solids will then sink to the bottom. At this stage gently pour the clarified butter over the chicken liver pâté, being careful not to allow the remaining milk solids in the jug to come out. Then garnish with a sprinkle of thyme leaves. Cover and store in the fridge until ready to serve.

This pâté is fantastic smeared on lightly toasted sourdough bread or with Prue's treacle bread (see page 193) and my chilli jam (see page 166).

CHEF'S TIPS

✦ Use this pâté to fill mini pastry casings and serve as a decadent canapé.

✦ This recipe will make enough for about 6 small ramekins or a 1kg loaf tin.

✦ You can freeze any unused pâté.

LEMON SOLE WITH GARLIC, CHILLI PRAWNS AND CREAMY MASH

I absolutely love the simplicity of lemon sole. It's widely available and it isn't too expensive. It doesn't need much cooking and the results are exquisite. You could replace the chilli prawns with beautiful fresh mussels.

prep: 10 minutes ✦ **marinate**: 2 hours ✦ **cook**: 30 minutes ✦ **serves**: 4

FOR THE SOLE

4 large fillets of lemon sole (or 8 small)

1 tbsp extra virgin olive oil

1 tbsp chopped fresh sage or tarragon

salt and freshly cracked black pepper

FOR THE CREAMY MASH

8 medium potatoes, peeled

100g butter

150ml cream

150ml milk

1 tbsp mayonnaise

pinch of freshly grated nutmeg

salt and freshly cracked black pepper

FOR THE BÉARNAISE SAUCE

2 small banana shallots, finely chopped

3 tbsp water

4 tbsp dry white wine

2 tbsp white wine vinegar

3 large free-range egg yolks, lightly beaten

200g unsalted butter, softened

3 tsp finely chopped fresh tarragon leaves

2 tsp finely chopped fresh chervil

salt and freshly cracked black pepper, to taste

Trim the sole and remove the bones.

In a food processor, blend the olive oil, chopped sage (or tarragon), salt and pepper. Drizzle over the lemon sole. Cover and transfer to the fridge to marinate for at least 2 hours.

Boil the potatoes until cooked. Mash the potatoes and add butter, milk, mayonnaise and cream and mix well to combine. Season with salt, pepper and nutmeg. Cover and keep warm in an oven preheated to 70°C fan/110°C/gas mark ¼.

To make the béarnaise sauce, place the shallots, water, wine and vinegar in a small saucepan and bring to the boil. Cook for three minutes or until the liquid has reduced by half. Transfer the mixture to a small metal (or heatproof) bowl and allow to cool for 5 minutes. Then place the bowl over a pan of simmering water, to create a bain-marie. Add the egg yolks one at a time and, using a hand blender, blend until combined. Add the softened butter 50g at a time, whisking constantly, until the sauce has thickened. Do this slowly so that the sauce does not curdle. Finally, add the tarragon and chervil, remove from the heat, and season with salt and pepper. The sauce can be gently reheated by placing the bowl over a pan of simmering water and stirring continuously until heated through. Once again, do not introduce too much heat or the sauce will split.

Preheat the oven to 160°C fan/180°C/gas mark 4.

To a hot frying pan, add the olive oil and butter. Once the butter has melted, lightly sauté the garlic and chilli for 1 minute. Add the prawns and cook for 2 minutes. Lightly season with salt and

1 tbsp olive oil

knob butter

2 garlic cloves, finely chopped

1 chilli, finely chopped

8 large prawns

pepper. Remove from the heat.

On a parchment-lined baking tray, lay out the sole fillets with at least 1 inch between each one. Bake for 3 to 5 minutes or until cooked.

To serve, place some mashed potato in the middle of the plate, top with a lemon sole fillet and then the prawns.

DAUPHINOISE POTATOES

◆◆◆

Gratin dauphinoise is a traditional regional French dish usually made with potatoes and crème fraîche, but I use milk and cream. It is originally from the historic Dauphiné region in south-east France. There are many variants of the name of the dish, including pommes de terre dauphinoise, potatoes à la dauphinoise and gratin de pommes à la Dauphinoise. For my version I use uncooked potatoes.

prep: 30 minutes ✦ **cook**: 1 hour ✦ **serves**: 12

100g butter

500ml milk

500ml double cream

2 tsp salt

2 tsp freshly cracked pepper

1 sprig of fresh thyme

3 whole garlic cloves, peeled

1 tsp freshly grated nutmeg

8 large potatoes, sliced into 5mm slices

1 onion, sliced into rings

170g Cheddar cheese, grated

YOU WILL ALSO NEED

32cm x 22cm baking tin or casserole dish

Preheat the oven to 200°C fan/220°C/gas mark 7. Butter the baking tin.

In a medium-sized saucepan, melt the butter over medium heat. Pour in the milk and cream. Season with the salt and pepper. Add the thyme, garlic and nutmeg and whisk for 5 minutes. Remove from the heat and allow to sit and infuse for 10 minutes. Strain the liquid and reserve.

Layer half of the potato and onion slices into the bottom of the prepared baking tin or casserole dish and pour over half the milk-and-cream mixture. Sprinkle with half the grated cheese and then add the remaining potato and onion slices. Pour over the rest of the milk-and-cream mixture. Finally, sprinkle over the remaining cheese. Cover with tin foil.

Bake for 50 minutes in the preheated oven. Remove foil and continue baking for a further 10 minutes, until the top is golden and bubbling.

CHEF'S TIP

✦ For best results, cook in advance and refrigerate overnight. Then cut the dauphinoise potatoes into 8cm x 7cm slices (approx). Cover with tin foil and reheat in an oven preheated to 160°C fan/180°C/gas mark 4 for 30 minutes or until warmed through. Remove the foil, sprinkle over some more cheese and bake for a further 10 minutes.

CHICKEN WITH WHITE WINE AND TARRAGON

◆◆

This is an elegant dish bursting with flavour. The chicken is so moist and incredibly succulent. Fresh tarragon is a beautifully aromatic herb, reminiscent of anise, and it works wonderfully with chicken.

prep: 10 minutes ✦ **marinate**: 40 minutes or overnight ✦ **cook**: 30 minutes ✦ **serves**: 6–8

6 free-range chicken breasts, trimmed

FOR THE MARINADE

150ml extra virgin olive oil

juice of 1 lemon

2 tbsp chopped fresh tarragon

1 tsp each salt and freshly cracked black pepper

FOR THE WHITE SAUCE

50g butter

50g plain flour

100ml white wine

250ml chicken stock

100ml milk

2 tsp freshly grated nutmeg

salt and freshly cracked black pepper

250ml cream

TO SERVE

rice or couscous

Cut the chicken into bite-size pieces. In a food processor, prepare the marinade by blending the olive oil, lemon juice, tarragon, salt and pepper. Place the chicken into a bowl and pour over the marinade, making sure the chicken is well coated. Cover and refrigerate for a minimum of 40 minutes but overnight if you can.

Remove the chicken from the fridge and allow to stand at room temperature while you prepare the sauce. Melt the butter in a large heavy-bottomed saucepan over a medium heat. Add the flour as if you were making a basic white sauce. When the mixture begins to bubble, add a little wine. Continue to mix while adding the rest of the wine. Cook for up to 2 minutes over a medium heat or until the mixture becomes very sticky. Begin to add the stock, little by little. Then add the milk, and continue to cook the mixture for up to 10 minutes. It is important that the flour is cooked and that the acidic smell/taste of the wine has evaporated. Add the grated nutmeg and salt and pepper to season.

Add in the chicken and poach for 10 minutes or until the chicken is cooked through. To test, remove one piece of chicken and cut in half. If it's at all pink, continue cooking for a further 5 minutes. When you're certain the chicken is cooked through, add the cream and cook for a further 5 minutes over a medium heat.

Serve with couscous or fluffy steamed rice.

◆◆

CHEF'S TIP

✦ Try not to overcook the chicken. It takes only around 10 minutes to poach the chicken pieces, and the smaller the pieces, the quicker they will cook. This dish is also great reheated. If you don't like tarragon, you can replace it with sage or a herb of your choice.

SLOW COOKED SPICED PORK BELLY AND CARAMELISED APPLES

◆◆◆

This is a great dish to serve on a large serving platter to share, allowing your guests to break off chunks of belly, or you can shred the flesh. You can also serve this as a starter in 6cm square cubes or larger, if desired. This recipe shows you how to serve the pork belly as a starter, served with caramelised apples and a spiced jus.

prep: 10 minutes ◆ **marinate**: overnight ◆ **cook**: 5 hours ◆ **serves**: 10 (as a starter)

FOR THE MARINADE

3 tbsp Chinese 5 spice powder

FOR THE PORK

3kg boneless belly of pork

12 garlic cloves, peeled

3 tsp cloves

3 tsp all spice berries

2 medium onions, peeled and quartered

4 baby new potatoes

4 carrots, peeled and quartered

3 tbsp tamarind paste (blitz this in a food processor)

4 tsp chipotle purée

5 tbsp soy sauce

6 tbsp balsamic vinegar

8 tbsp demerara sugar

5 chipotle chillies, dried or fresh

2 litres beef stock

To marinate the pork, massage the 5 spice powder into the skin on both sides of the pork belly. Place in an airtight container and refrigerate overnight.

Place the marinated pork in a large heat-proof casserole pot. Add all the remaining ingredients. Cook over a high heat on the hob for 25 minutes, and then reduce the heat to medium and leave to bubble away gently for 35 minutes, covered.

Preheat the oven to 120°C fan/140°C/gas mark 1.

Place the casserole pot in the preheated oven, and leave to slow cook for 4 hours. Remove from oven and drain the pork, retaining the cooking liquid and vegetables for later. Place the pork on a baking tray. Cover with tin foil and using something heavy, such as a cookery book or heavy saucepan, compress the cooked pork belly. Allow to cool and then refrigerate for 3–4 hours, or overnight for the best results.

Strain the hot cooking liquid/stock from the pork into a smaller saucepan. Discard the vegetables. Bring the stock to the boil over a high heat, and then reduce to medium and allow to simmer until the liquid has reduced by 40–50 per cent. The liquid, or jus, should now be syrupy in consistency.

Remove the pork from the fridge and remove the skin with a sharp knife. Do not remove too much of the fat as this has incredible flavour. Cut the meat into 5cm cubes or 200g portions, ready for serving. You can serve this hot or cold. If serving hot, place in a preheated oven (200°C fan/220°C/gas mark 7) for 15 minutes. Keep warm until ready to serve.

Continued overleaf

2 Bramley apples, peeled and cored

50g butter

2 tbsp caster sugar

juice and zest of 1 lemon

1 tbsp Cointreau or any sweet liqueur

TO SERVE

chilli jam (see recipe on page 166)

For the caramelised apples, cut the peeled and cored apples into large segments. Place the butter in a shallow frying pan. Add the apples, sugar and lemon zest and juice. Lightly fry for 1 minute. Add the liqueur. Continue cooking for a further 1–2 minutes. Remove from the heat.

On a dinner plate, place one tablespoon of chilli jam (or similar) in the middle of the plate. With the back of the spoon, smear the chilli jam from left to right. Gently place the cube of pork belly in the middle of the plate and carefully drizzle 2 tablespoons of the jus over the dish. Serve immediately with the caramelised apples.

Alternatively, place the pork belly on a large serving platter with baby new potatoes, and roasted root vegetables. Garnish with the caramelised apples and serve the hot jus in a jug.

CHEF'S TIPS

+ Chinese 5 spice powder is an aromatic blend of star anise, cloves, fennel seeds, Sichuan pepper and Chinese cinnamon.

+ If you can't source the dried chipotle chillies you can use fresh chillies instead.

+ You can replace the pork belly with a similar weight of brisket of beef. When the beef cools, shred it into 70g portions. Then simply place a 6cm x 3cm circular cookie cutter on a starter plate, fill with the shredded beef and carefully remove the cutter, leaving a perfectly round starter portion. Drizzle with the jus. The chilli jam also goes really well with this.

BEEF WELLINGTON

❖❖❖

The origin of the name "beef Wellington" is unclear. There is a theory that suggests beef Wellington is named after Arthur Wellesley, 1st Duke of Wellington. However, the late, great Clarissa Dickson Wright is of a different opinion. When she was introducing a recipe for beef Wellington, she claimed, "This dish has nothing to do with that splendid hero, the Duke of Wellington. It was invented for a civic reception in Wellington, New Zealand, but it is a splendid addition to any party." No matter what the origin, this dish is divine and must be tried.

prep: 40 minutes ✦ **cook**: 25 minutes ✦ **serves**: 6–8

1.3kg piece of beef fillet (about 30cm in length)

salt and freshly cracked black pepper

a little olive oil

15g unsalted butter

1 packet ready-rolled (all butter) puff pastry

6 shop-bought potato cakes

175g chicken liver pâté (see recipe on page 97)

1 small egg, beaten

FOR THE DUXELLE MUSHROOM STUFFING

55g unsalted butter

150g shallots, peeled and finely diced

2 garlic cloves, chopped

2 tsp chopped fresh thyme

250g flat cap mushrooms, chopped

3 tbsp double cream

salt and freshly ground black pepper

Season the beef with salt and pepper. Heat the oil and butter in a large non-stick frying pan. When hot add the seasoned beef and seal on all sides for 1½ to 2 minutes on each side until evenly browned all over. Remove from the pan and allow to cool completely on a wire rack, collecting the lovely juices in a tray underneath. Reserve the juices to add to the jus (if using).

To make the duxelle stuffing, add the butter to the same frying pan. When it's hot and foaming, add the diced shallot, garlic and thyme and cook until the shallots and garlic are softened and golden. Add the mushrooms and season with salt and pepper. Cook for a further 5 minutes or until all the liquid evaporates. Stir in the cream. Continue to cook over a low heat until reduced to your desired consistency (it should be quite thick). Set aside to cool completely.

Preheat the oven to 210°C fan/230°C/gas mark 8.

Roll out the pastry on a well-floured surface. You want to roll it out large enough to fit the piece of beef. Lay three of the potato cakes in the centre of the pastry, slightly overlapping. Spread a layer of chicken liver pâté across the centre of the potato cakes (roughly the same width as your fillet of beef).

Place the beef directly onto the potato cakes. The potato cakes soak up any excess cooking liquid, ensuring that the pastry does not split.

Continued overleaf

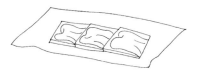

Spread the duxelle stuffing across the top of the beef. Any leftover mushrooms can be reheated and served with the dish. Fold both sides of the pastry up and over the beef, joining the two ends together over the centre of the fillet, and crimp with a fork. Press tightly when handling the pastry. It's important not to have any air pockets. The package needs to be fairly tight. Trim the pastry if necessary. Tuck the ends over and crimp with a fork.

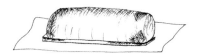

Brush the edges with a little egg wash. Place the Wellington seam side down on a large baking tray, lined with parchment. Use enough parchment to overlap the sides, so that it can be easily lifted out after cooking. Decorate the top with extra pastry if desired and then brush all over with the beaten egg. With a small knife, make 3 small incisions along the middle of the parcel. This allows the beef to breathe and ensures that the pastry does not split or crack. Brush again with egg wash.

Place in the hot oven for 10 minutes, and then reduce the heat to 170°C fan/190°C/gas mark 5 and continue to cook for another 10–15 minutes or until the pastry is golden.

Remove from the oven to a carving board and allow to rest for 5 minutes before carving into thick slices. Oh, but make sure that you show it off to your guests before carving. It will deserve a round of applause!

Slice the Wellington carefully on a warm baking tray. If it breaks, you can tidy it up. Using a spatula, carefully lift it and place on the middle of the plate you are serving it on.

Serve with creamy mash (see recipe on page 98), seasonal vegetables and a drizzle of beef jus (see recipe on page 32).

CHEF'S TIPS

+ You can refrigerate the beef Wellington for 20 minutes before cooking, to firm the pastry up further.
+ Another interesting variation is to add 100g of escalopes de foie gras de canard through the chicken liver pâté. I picked this tip up from Pete in Fallon & Byrne, which has to be Dublin's best food hall; in fact, Europe's best food hall. Jennifer, I want a bottle of your finest for that plug.

LEMON TART

❖❖❖

Lemon tart is always a firm favourite. Don't get too worried about the process, as it's relatively simple. If you like, you can double the amount of pastry and freeze half of it for the next time. You can also cheat and use shop-bought pastry or a ready-to-go pastry case, which is slightly naughty but perfectly acceptable if you're not comfortable making your own pastry.

prep: 1 hour ✦ **cook**: 50 minutes ✦ **serves**: 8

FOR THE PASTRY

250g plain flour

110g chilled butter, diced

75g icing sugar

3 free-range egg yolks

1 free-range egg, lightly beaten

FOR THE LEMON CURD FILLING

5 organic or free-range eggs

160g caster sugar

85ml lemon juice

2 tbsp freshly grated lemon zest

150ml double cream

1 tsp vanilla extract

TO SERVE

icing sugar, to dust

fresh berries (optional)

YOU WILL ALSO NEED

1 x 24cm loose-bottomed tart tin

baking beans (or any uncooked large
    pulses or beans)

To make the pastry, sieve the flour into a mixing bowl and rub in the butter until the mixture resembles fine breadcrumbs. Sprinkle in the sugar, add the egg yolks, and then mix to form the dough. Press the mixture together to form a rounded shape. Remove from the bowl, and on a lightly floured surface knead the pastry gently. Do not overwork it. Flatten the pastry slightly and wrap in cling film. Allow to rest in the fridge for up to 1 hour.

Preheat the oven to 150°C fan/170°C/gas mark 3.

Roll out the pastry on a floured surface. Use the 24cm loose-bottomed baking tin as a template to get the size right. Roll the pastry over the rolling pin and then unroll it over the baking tin. Gently tuck the pastry into the corners and up the sides of the tin. Press it against the sides with your thumbs very gently. Cut off any excess pastry. Prick the base a few times with a fork, and then line the pastry with a sheet of greaseproof paper and pour in some baking beans (or any uncooked large pulses or beans). Place in the fridge for 30 minutes. Transfer to the preheated oven to "blind bake" for about 15 minutes. Then remove the beans and parchment, brush the pastry with a little lightly beaten egg and return to the oven until very lightly coloured, about 25 minutes.

While the pastry is blind baking in the oven, you can make the lemon curd filling. Place the eggs, sugar, lemon juice and zest in a large bowl, and whisk for a few seconds. Add the cream and vanilla extract and whisk them in. Place the mixture in the fridge until you are ready to use it.

Pour the lemon curd into a saucepan and warm very gently (this is to speed up the cooking time of the tart), but be very careful not to overheat the lemon curd, or it will scramble. It will take just 3–4 minutes to get the cooking process going.

- You can use small pastry cases to make individual tarts. Just reduce the baking time to about 8 minutes.
- Always taste the lemon curd filling to ensure that the balance of lemon juice/zest and sugar is correct.

Increase the oven temperature to 160°C fan/180°C/gas mark 4.

Pour the warm lemon curd mixture into the blind-baked (or ready-made) pastry case and bake for 25 minutes, or until barely set. There should still be a slight wobble in the middle. Remove from the oven and leave to cool for at least 1 hour.

Remove from tin and place on a serving plate. Dredge with icing sugar and dot with fresh berries to serve.

CRÈME BRÛLÉE

❖❖❖

My mum used to make crème caramel when we were children. It was such a treat but it's fairly time consuming to make. This classic crème brûlée is so quick and easy to prepare and doesn't require cooking in the oven or in a bain-marie. Once the custard is made, it goes straight into the fridge. I recently made 280 in ramekins for a wedding. The comforting thing with this recipe is that it sets every time.

prep: 5 minutes ✦ **cook**: 10 minutes ✦ **refrigerate**: 3–24 hours ✦ **serves**: 5

4 large organic egg yolks

50g caster sugar

300ml double cream

100ml milk

1 vanilla pod or 2 tsp vanilla extract

10 tsp demerara sugar

2 tsp ground cinnamon (optional)

TO SERVE

fresh berries

5 leaves fresh mint

YOU WILL ALSO NEED

5 large ramekins (100ml, 6.5cm diameter x 5.5cm depth)

In a bowl, beat together the egg yolks and caster sugar using a whisk.

Pour the cream and milk into a saucepan. If you are using a vanilla pod, first you will need to split the pod lengthwise. Then, using a paring knife, scrape the seeds from both sides of the pod and add the seeds and the scraped pod to the cream and milk. If you're not using the pod, you can simply add the vanilla extract to the cream and milk.

Heat the milk gently over a medium heat until it starts to form a skin. Do not allow it to boil. Remove from the heat and slowly pour it over the egg mixture, whisking constantly.

Return the mix to the saucepan and heat gently over a low to medium heat, stirring constantly until the custard is thick enough to coat the back of a wooden spoon.

Remove from the heat and pour through a fine strainer into a jug. This will remove the vanilla pod and any lumps.

If the custard becomes lumpy or if it curdles when cooking, remove from the heat immediately and pour into a glass bowl and place directly into another bowl of ice-cold water, whilst whisking the custard. This should remove any lumps. Then strain again.

Divide the custard between the 5 ramekins and leave to cool. Cover and refrigerate overnight.

When ready to serve, evenly sprinkle 1 to 2 teaspoons of demerara sugar over each crème brûlée. If you like you can mix the cinnamon in with the sugar beforehand. If you have a chef's blowtorch, set it to full heat and caramelise the sugar. Don't hold it too close as the sugar will burn. Alternatively place the ramekins under a hot grill for up to 30 seconds.

Once the caramel topping has cooled and set, serve immediately with fresh berries and a mint leaf.

CHEF'S TIP

✦ To make chocolate crème brûlée, add 4 tsp cocoa powder to the milk and cream when the mixture is infusing with the vanilla pod.

RICH CHOCOLATE CAKE

✦✦✦

I was recently asked to prepare a chocolate cake for a client. They wanted a beautifully opulent and moist chocolate cake with layers of the richest chocolate ganache and a fruit and cream filling. After experimenting with a few different combinations, I came up with this cake that is simply lovely. Interestingly, fresh pineapple works really well in the filling with the strawberries.

prep: 20 minutes ✦ **cook**: 1 hour 20 minutes ✦ **serves**: 8–14

FOR THE CAKE

300g good quality dark chocolate (70 per cent cocoa solids), broken into pieces

300g butter, cubed

210g self-raising flour

150g plain flour

3 tsp baking powder

300g light muscovado sugar

300g caster sugar

40g cocoa powder

6 large free-range eggs, separated

½ tbsp vanilla extract

100ml buttermilk

1 tbsp instant coffee granules

125ml tepid water

2 tsp bicarbonate of soda (baking soda)

50ml Tia Maria, or liqueur of your choice

FOR THE GANACHE

200g good quality dark chocolate, (70 per cent cocoa solids)

200g butter, softened

250ml cream

2 tbsp caster sugar

shot of Tia Maria liqueur

Preheat the oven to 140°C fan/160°C/gas mark 3.

To prepare the cake, put the chocolate pieces and cubed butter into a small Pyrex bowl. Place over a medium, heavy-based saucepan ¾ filled with water. Over a low heat, warm the chocolate and butter until they have just melted, and then remove from the heat.

While the chocolate is cooling, mix the self-raising flour, plain flour, baking powder, light muscovado sugar, caster sugar and cocoa powder in a mixing bowl, using your fingers to get rid of any lumps.

Beat the egg yolks and vanilla extract in a bowl until creamy in texture, and then stir in the buttermilk. Now pour the melted chocolate mixture and the egg mixture into the flour, stirring just until everything is well combined and you have a smooth but quite runny consistency.

In a separate bowl, whisk the egg whites until they form stiff peaks. Gradually fold this into the cake mixture.

Dissolve the instant coffee granules in 125ml tepid water, and then add the bicarbonate of soda (baking soda). After 3 minutes, combine this with the cake mixture.

Pour the cake mixture into the tin and bake for about 1 hour 20 minutes. After that time remove the cake from the oven and test to see if it is cooked by pushing a skewer into the centre. The skewer should come out clean and the top of the cake should feel firm (don't worry if it cracks a bit). Leave to cool in the tin. It may dip slightly and that's fine. Then turn out onto a wire rack to cool completely.

When the cake is cold, cut it horizontally in two.

grated chocolate

chocolate flakes

fresh strawberries, raspberries, pineapple
  or cherries

apricot jam

250ml whipped cream, if desired

1 x 24cm round cake tin, lined

To make the ganache, chop the chocolate into small pieces and tip into a bowl with the butter. Place the bowl on top of a pot of gently simmering water. Pour the cream into a pan, add 2 tablespoons of caster sugar, and heat to just below boiling point. Remove from the heat and pour over the chocolate. Add the Tia Maria and stir until the chocolate has melted and the mixture is smooth. Then remove from the bain-marie and leave to cool.

To assemble the cake, sandwich the layers together with apricot jam, just a little bit of the ganache, whipped cream, and your preferred fruit. Pour the rest of the ganache over the cake, letting it drip decadently down the sides, and smooth the top with a palette knife. Decorate with grated chocolate or a pile of chocolate flakes, and fresh fruit if you like.

This cake will keep, and stay moist and gooey, for 3–4 days in an airtight container.

ELEGANT DINNER PARTY

FLAVOUR SENSATIONS

Arancini risotto balls with wild mushrooms
Garlic chilli prawns
Beef Wellington
Crème brûlée

Wine suggestions

White: a dry full-bodied Riesling ✦ Red: a full-bodied wine like an Australian Grenache or a Châteauneuf-style wine

FABULOUS FEAST

Fillet of beef with horseradish
Slow cooked spiced pork belly and caramelised apples
Chicken with white wine and tarragon
Lemon tart

Wine suggestions

White: a big bold Chardonnay from Burgundy or Australia ✦ Red: a hearty Grenache or Syrah from the south of France

FRESH FROM THE SEA

Crab and apple bites
Summer smoked haddock mousse
Lemon sole with garlic, chilli prawns and creamy mash
Rich chocolate cake

Wine suggestions

White: a Touraine Sauvignon or New Zealand Sauvignon or a Sancerre or Pouilly Fumé from Loire

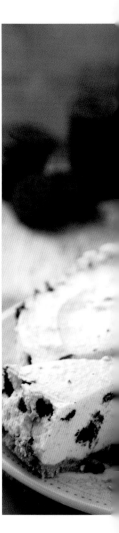

THE BIG FEAST

This is another of my favourite ways to entertain. I love to have large groups of friends over and lay out a tempting and varied spread for everyone to dig in to. And if the sun shines and you can be out in the garden, all the better! A mix of cold and hot food gives your guests plenty of choice. The thing to remember is that you don't have to worry that the number of portions for each dish matches the number of guests. A good selection of colour, variety and flavour is the key thing here. Many of these dishes can be prepared in advance, too, so as long as you're a little organised, the prep shouldn't be a big deal. If you're catering for more than 15 guests, you might think about laying the dishes out in sections — with a seafood counter, a salad bar, and separate areas for the hot food and dessert. Make sure to have handwritten descriptions beside each dish so guests know what they're choosing.

BEEF TOMATO SALAD WITH MUSTARD DRESSING

This salad is unusual but it's always a firm favourite. It's refreshing and it has a lovely sharp flavour enhanced by the fresh mint and Dijon mustard.

prep: 5 minutes ✦ **serves**: 2–4

3 beef tomatoes

3 spring onions

FOR THE DRESSING

1 tsp Dijon mustard

2 tsp tarragon vinegar or white wine vinegar

2 tbsp olive oil

pinch brown sugar

2 tsp finely chopped fresh mint

salt and freshly cracked black pepper

Turn the tomatoes on their side and cut them into slices about 5cm thick. Arrange in overlapping, concentric circles on a plate.

Trim and clean the spring onions. Cut in half lengthways and then slice on the diagonal. Scatter over the tomatoes.

Whisk all the dressing ingredients together in a jug and drizzle over the salad.

Serve immediately with crusty white bread.

CHEF'S TIP

✦ This salad is also lovely served with sliced mozzarella. If you like, you can garnish the salad with sprigs of mint as well.

ASIAN CHICKEN NOODLE SOUP

✦✦✦

I have a great system to make sure that the quantities of noodles and shredded chicken are exactly the same for everyone when you serve this soup. Don't add the noodles or shredded chicken to the stockpot. Instead prepare the noodles separately. Drain and set aside. Do the same with the shredded chicken. When serving, place a small amount of noodles in the soup bowl, followed by one tablespoon of shredded chicken. Then pour the soup over this and serve immediately

prep: 10 minutes ✦ **cook**: 50 minutes ✦ **serves**: 6–8

FOR THE ASIAN STOCK

1½ litres chicken stock

5 cardamom pods, toasted until fragrant

2 cinnamon sticks

4 cloves of garlic, peeled and roughly chopped

10 Kaffir lime leaves, deveined and sliced into thin strips

2 stalks of lemongrass, bruised and finely chopped

5cm piece of fresh ginger, peeled and roughly chopped

2 small chilli peppers, roughly chopped in 3

FOR THE SOUP

500ml chicken stock, to poach the chicken breasts

2 free-range chicken breasts

50ml sunflower/vegetable oil

2 sticks of celery, peeled (to remove strings) and diced

2 carrots, peeled and very finely diced

1 onion, peeled and finely diced

1 tbsp fish sauce (nam pla)

juice of ½ lime

1 tbsp caster sugar

100g uncooked rice noodles

3 tsp freshly cracked black pepper, or to taste

To prepare the stock, bring 1½ litres of chicken stock to the boil in a stockpot or large saucepan. Then add the cardamom pods, cinnamon sticks, garlic, Kaffir lime leaves, lemongrass, ginger and chilli peppers. Bring to the boil and then simmer for 20 minutes. Remove from the heat. Once cool, pass through a sieve. Retain the liquid and discard the remaining ingredients.

To prepare the soup, bring 500ml chicken stock to the boil and then reduce the heat and gently poach the whole chicken breasts for 10–15 minutes. Remove from the heat, drain and allow the chicken breasts to cool. When cool, shred the chicken. Discard the poaching liquid.

Place a large pot over a medium heat, add the oil and sauté the celery, carrots and onion for 5 minutes. Add the Asian stock, then add the shredded chicken and warm through for further a 5 minutes. Add the fish sauce, lime juice, sugar and rice noodles and cook for a further 5 minutes (or according to the pack instructions) over a low to medium heat. Taste and add more sugar, lime juice and freshly cracked black pepper if you like.

Serve immediately with crusty bread.

✦✦✦

CHEF'S TIPS

✦ There are lots of wonderful variations of this recipe. You can add 100ml coconut milk if you like a creamier soup. A handful of button mushrooms would also work really well added at the same time as the chicken.

✦ Run a vegetable peeler over the celery to remove the tough strings.

REFRIED BEANS (OR BLACK BEAN SOUP)

Black beans are typically used in Latin American cuisine. They are high in protein and low in fat. They are also a great source of soluble fibre. The recipe for this soup came about by accident when I was making refried beans for a Mexican dish. I had some left over and decided to make a soup using exactly the same ingredients, and then just added some vegetable stock. It worked well and is really very fragrant.

prep: 5 minutes ✦ **cook**: 20 minutes ✦ **serves**: 4

1 tbsp olive oil

3 garlic cloves, peeled and finely chopped

1 medium onion, peeled and finely chopped

2 tomatoes, deseeded and chopped small

400g tin black beans, drained

1 tbsp chopped fresh oregano (½ tbsp dried is also fine)

100ml vegetable stock

TO MAKE THE SOUP

1 litre vegetable stock

salt and freshly cracked black pepper, to taste

In a heavy-bottomed saucepan, sauté the onions and garlic over a low heat with the olive oil for 5 minutes. Add the tomatoes, black beans, oregano and stock. Sauté for a further 15 minutes. Taste and season with salt and pepper if needed.

Serve hot with crusty bread or in a burrito.

This also makes a great soup. After you've sautéed the ingredients just add 1 litre of vegetable stock and blend to your preferred consistency using a hand blender. Cook for a further 10 minutes.

PAUL ARNOLD'S PORK SOUVLAKI WITH TZATZIKI

◆◆◆

Souvlaki (pronounced soo-vlah-kee) is the Greek version of a kebab. The term literally means "made of lamb" and is used to describe little skewers of meat marinated in red wine and herbs and then grilled. It's served with a delicious Greek minted cucumber dip called tzatziki. We use pork in this recipe but you can replace it with lamb if you like. Oh, and a note just for Paul: this is my tzatziki recipe — hands off!

prep: 30 minutes ◆ **marinate**: 3–24 hours ◆ **cook**: 8–10 minutes ◆ **serves**: 4

1kg pork tenderloin (pork steak), trimmed and cut into 2.5cm cubes

FOR THE MARINADE

100ml extra virgin olive oil

100ml red wine

1 red onion, peeled and cut into wedges

2 garlic cloves, peeled and finely diced

juice of 1 lemon

2 tbsp red wine vinegar

1 tbsp dried oregano

1 tbsp mint

1 tbsp thyme

salt and freshly cracked black pepper

FOR THE TZATZIKI

1 cucumber, peeled, deseeded and grated

2 garlic cloves

2 tsp rock salt

300ml natural Greek-style yogurt

2 tbsp chopped fresh mint

cracked black pepper, to taste

1 tbsp extra virgin olive oil (optional)

½ tsp red wine vinegar (optional)

YOU WILL ALSO NEED

8 skewers

To marinate the meat, put the pork in a large bowl and add in all the marinade ingredients. Turn over the meat in the marinade to ensure it is well coated in the liquid. Cover and leave to marinate for at least 3 hours in the fridge, but overnight is preferable to achieve the best results.

To make the tzatziki, place the cucumber in a strainer or colander. Sprinkle with salt and leave for 30 minutes. Rinse, drain and dry with kitchen paper. With the flat side of a chef's knife, mash the garlic to a paste with 1 teaspoon of rock salt.

Mix the yogurt, garlic, mint and cucumber in a bowl. Add pepper and salt, to taste. Add the optional ingredients, if desired. Mix well to combine. Cover and chill.

If you are using wooden skewers, first soak them in water for 20 minutes so that they do not burn under the grill.

Thread the pork onto the skewers and grill for 8–10 minutes or until cooked, turning regularly to make sure the meat is browned on all sides. Brush with the rest of the marinade as they cook.

Serve with warm pittas, tzatziki and olives.

◆◆◆

CHEF'S TIP

◆ Be careful not to add too much salt to the tzatziki.

SPICED COLESLAW

This is such a simple recipe and it can be prepared in minutes. If you have a food processor with a grating blade, it makes quick work of grating or shredding the vegetables.

prep: 15 minutes ✦ **serves**: 12

100g currants

200ml veg stock

400g mayonnaise (see recipe for
 homemade mayonnaise on page 136)

200ml buttermilk

1 tbsp caster sugar

1 large white cabbage, shredded

4 small red onions, peeled and shredded

6 large carrots, peeled and shredded

1 tbsp celery seeds, toasted

2 tbsp black mustard seeds, toasted

salt and freshly cracked pepper

Soak the currants in the vegetable stock for 10 minutes. Drain and discard the stock.

Put the mayonnaise, buttermilk and caster sugar in the bowl of a food processor and blitz to a smooth paste. Season with salt and freshly cracked pepper.

Add all the remaining ingredients to a mixing bowl. Pour the mayonnaise mixture over and mix thoroughly with a spoon. You can make the coleslaw as wet or dry as you like by using more or less of the mayonnaise mixture. Season to taste.

This is delicious served with cold meats or anything cooked on the barbecue.

CHEF'S TIP

+   To toast spices, simply place a pan over a medium heat, and once hot add the spices to the dry pan and let them toast until they become fragrant (about 30 seconds). This little trick really boosts the flavour of dry spices.

AIDAN MEYLER'S SPICY CHICKEN BAKE

My friend Aidan knows his food. He has worked in some amazing restaurants over the years, including the famous Michelin-starred l'Ecrivain in Dublin, which is owned by my friends Derry and Sallyanne Clarke. I had not regarded Aidan as a passionate cook, but this recipe has proven me very wrong. For lovers of Buffalo chicken wings in hot sauce, this one is a must. This is an all-in-one no-mess party dipping bowl with all the flavours of your favourite hot wings combined!

prep: 20 minutes ✦ **cook**: 50 minutes ✦ **serves**: 10

FOR THE BLUE CHEESE SAUCE

450g blue cheese

200ml mayonnaise

1 garlic clove, crushed

juice of ½ lemon

250ml sour cream

50ml milk, if required

FOR THE CHICKEN

1 roast chicken, cooled and with all the meat removed from the bone, skin discarded

450g cream cheese

2 tsp celery salt or toasted celery seeds

1 tsp cayenne

100ml Louisiana Hot Sauce, or any hot chilli sauce

220g breadcrumbs

225g Parmesan cheese, grated

To make the blue cheese sauce, place half of the blue cheese in a large mixing bowl. Add the mayonnaise, garlic, lemon juice and sour cream and blend using a hand blender. You may need to add a little milk to loosen it up. When completely blended and smooth, add the remaining blue cheese, roughly crumbled, so that you end up with a lumpy sauce.

Next, place the roast chicken meat in a large bowl. In a separate bowl mix the cream cheese, celery salt and cayenne. Add this to the chicken. Mix well with a spatula and then add the hot sauce and half of the blue cheese sauce. Mix gently with a spatula until the chicken is completly coated in the sauce. Taste and add more hot sauce and/or cayenne pepper until it is as hot as you like! I don't add salt because the blue cheese is salty enough that it comes through.

Preheat the oven to 160°C fan/180°C/gas mark 4.

Add in almost all of the rest of the blue cheese sauce but hold back a little for dressing later. Place the mixture in a casserole dish, cover with a mixture of breadcrumbs and grated Parmesan and bake in the oven for 40 minutes. Then increase the oven to 170°C fan/190°C/gas mark 4 and cook for a further 10 minutes to achieve a lovely crisp, brown top.

Serve with a little more blue cheese sauce drizzled over the top. You can serve this with celery sticks, nachos, tortillas or even crusty bread on the side. And it's great served warm or at room temperature.

Enjoy!

Aidan

BBQ SPARE RIBS WITH MASHED POTATOES

Growing up on a pig farm, we always had a plentiful supply of all things pork-related, including ribs. My mum had a great recipe and she always served the ribs with lovely creamy mashed potatoes. My fondest memory of this dish goes back to 1990, when my friend Clive Williamson and I were heading off to our first music festival — Féile, affectionately known as the Trip to Tipp. We went off laden with our tents, camping stoves, sleeping bags and, more importantly, our supply of rashers and sausages. After a fantastic weekend of Van Morrison, The Saw Doctors, Meat Loaf, Mary Black and many more, we were collected by a great friend, Ciaran Carolan, in his Volkswagen Beetle and arrived home to be greeted with Mum's famous BBQ spare ribs and creamy mashed potatoes. They nearly outshone the festival!

prep: 25 minutes ✦ **cook**: 55 minutes ✦ **serves**: 8

2 racks of baby back pork ribs

FOR THE BARBECUE SAUCE

1 onion, peeled and finely diced

2 garlic cloves, peeled and finely diced

100ml red wine vinegar

150ml ketchup

1 x 400g tin of chopped tomatoes

4 tbsp tomato purée

100ml water

1 tsp Colman's Dry Mustard Powder

½ tsp chilli powder

2 tbsp Worcestershire sauce

1 tsp Tabasco

1 tbsp freshly squeezed lemon juice

1 tsp honey

2 tbsp brown sugar

1 tbsp paprika

1 tsp cayenne

3 tsp sea salt or 1 tsp table salt

1 tsp freshly cracked black pepper

1 bay leaf

TO SERVE

creamy mashed potatoes (see recipe on page 98)

Put 2 rib racks in a saucepan and cover with water. Boil the for 45 minutes. Remove from heat, drain the liquid and allow to cool.

To make the barbecue sauce, add a glug of oil to a frying pan over a medium heat and sauté the onions and garlic. Then set aside and allow to cool. Once cool, combine the sautéed onion and garlic with the remaining ingredients in a medium saucepan and mix until well combined. Cook over a high heat for 5 minutes and then reduce the heat to medium, cover and cook for a further 15 minutes. Remove the bay leaf and, using a hand blender, blend until you have a smooth sauce.

Preheat the oven to 180°C fan/200°C/gas mark 6. Place the ribs in a roasting tin. Pour over the barbecue sauce so that the ribs are well coated. Cover with tin foil and roast for 45 minutes. Remove the foil and cook for a further 10 minutes until dark and sticky and delicious.

Serve with creamy mashed potatoes. Serve either whole or as individual ribs.

CHEF'S TIP

✦ If you prefer less heat, simply add an extra tablespoon of honey to the barbecue sauce recipe and cook for a further 5 minutes.

CELERIAC REMOULADE

◆◆◆

My friend Ruth first introduced me to this root vegetable. I played around with a few variations, and came up with this lovely fresh recipe. It works really well served as a side dish with a selection of cold meats or a buffet menu. I have given you the recipe for homemade mayonnaise, but you can use a shop-bought jar if you prefer.

prep: 5 minutes ✦ **serves**: 6

FOR THE MAYONNAISE

2 free-range egg yolks

1 tbsp white wine vinegar

salt and freshly cracked black pepper

300ml sunflower oil

FOR THE CELERIAC REMOULADE

1 head celeriac, peeled, cored and grated

juice of 1 lemon

½ tsp celery seeds, toasted and crushed

½ tsp cumin seeds, toasted and crushed

2 tsp Dijon mustard

400ml mayonnaise

2 tbsp buttermilk

2 tbsp finely chopped flat leaf parsley

salt and freshly cracked black pepper

To make the mayonnaise, whisk the egg yolks and the white wine vinegar, either by hand or with an electric whisk. Very gradually whisk in the oil to make a thick and creamy mayonnaise. Season with salt and pepper. Transfer into an airtight jar and refrigerate until needed.

To make the remoulade, simply grate the celeriac into a large bowl. Combine the remaining ingredients in a food processor and then pour over the grated celeriac.

◆◆◆

CHEF'S TIP

✦ Homemade mayonnaise will keep perfectly well in an airtight container in the fridge for up to a week or more, depending on the freshness of the eggs used. I prefer to use sunflower or vegetable oil, as I find olive oil too strong and acidic. You can also add 1 finely chopped clove of garlic if you like. You can make the remoulade as wet or dry as you like. Just remember that it's more difficult to take the liquid out than to put it in. Just add more mayonnaise and buttermilk if it's too dry and drain the mixture if it's too wet.

BEEF BOURGUIGNON

◆◆◆

This dish originates from the Burgundy region of France. This method of slow cooking tenderises the beef beautifully. In Mastering the Art of French Cooking Julia Child describes sauté de boeuf à la Bourguignonne as "certainly one of the most delicious beef dishes concocted by man". I tend to agree, and so do my customers.

prep: 10 minutes ◆ **marinate:** 24 hours ◆ **cook:** 4 hours ◆ **serves:** 6

FOR THE MARINADE

1.5kg stewing beef, cubed

salt and freshly cracked black pepper

2 large carrots, peeled and each cut into 3 pieces

2 large onions, peeled and cut into chunks

5 garlic cloves, peeled but left whole

4 bay leaves

3 tbsp finely chopped fresh thyme

750ml red wine

FOR THE BOURGUIGNON

1 litre good beef stock

2 tbsp tomato purée

1 x 400g tin chopped tomatoes

peel of 1 orange, cut into strips

a good knob of butter

20 shallots, peeled but left whole (optional)

500g small button mushrooms, cleaned

200g rindless streaky rashers, roughly chopped

50g flour and 50g butter for the roux (optional)

TO SERVE

2 tbsp chopped fresh flat leaf parsley

To prepare the marinade, season the beef with salt and pepper and place into a plastic container with a lid or a large heavy-duty ziplock bag. Add the carrots, onions, garlic, bay leaves, thyme and red wine. Seal and refrigerate overnight.

Once marinated, place the beef and all the contents of the marinade into your largest oven-proof casserole pot. Bring up to the boil and add the beef stock, tomato purée, tin of tomatoes and orange peel. Cook over a high heat for 15 minutes, removing any scum from the top with a slotted spoon as it forms. Reduce the heat, cover and cook for a further 4 hours. Alternatively transfer into a preheated oven (160°C fan/180°C/gas mark 4) for at least 3½ hours.

In the meantime, using a large frying pan, sauté the whole shallots and button mushrooms in a knob of butter for approximately 5 minutes. Season with salt and pepper. Add these to the casserole pot of bourguignon 30 minutes before the end of the cooking time. Now fry off the streaky rashers and add those to the pot too.

Check the bourguignon for seasoning and add more if needed. Remove the orange peel and bay leaf. At this stage you can thicken the bourguignon following the instructions below, but if you prefer, you can skip that step and simply serve the bourguignon right now. It will still taste great.

To thicken the bourguignon, first prepare a roux by melting the butter in a small pan over a medium heat and slowly adding the flour, whisking constantly. Within 2–3 minutes the roux will take on a consistency of cake frosting. Remove the pan from the heat and let the roux cool.

CHEF'S TIP

+ This is a great one-pot wonder. Many people recommend that you should dry and sear the beef in advance of the slow cook. This is not necessary, as it is already bursting with flavour.

Drain the liquid from the bourguignon and pour it into a saucepan. Bring up to the boil and add in the roux, little by little, whisking constantly. The liquid should begin to thicken immediately. Continue to cook for about 3–4 minutes and ensure there are no lumps. Then pour this thickened sauce back into the bourguignon and serve immediately.

Serve with freshly chopped parsley.

MASCARPONE AND RICOTTA CHEESECAKE

I am really proud of this cheesecake. The light texture of the ricotta combined with the mascarpone produces a beautifully creamy dessert. It's quick and easy and doesn't require baking.

prep: 20 minutes ✦ **chill**: overnight ✦ **serves**: 8–12

FOR THE BASE

200g digestive biscuits

90g butter, softened

pinch of ground cinnamon

FOR THE TOPPING

6 gelatine sheets or 6 tsp powdered gelatine

350ml double cream, whipped

250g ricotta cheese

250g mascarpone cheese

75g caster sugar, or to desired taste

1 tbsp vanilla extract

8 Oreo biscuits

TO SERVE

icing sugar or cocoa powder, to dust (optional)

YOU WILL ALSO NEED

1 x 20cm spring-form cake tin, lined and greased

Add the base ingredients to a food processor and blitz until they come together as fine crumbs.

Line the cake tin with the base mixture and press down with the back of a spoon to compact it. Cover and refrigerate for 1 hour.

Prepare the sheets of gelatine by soaking in a bowl of cold water for 5 minutes, allowing them to swell slightly. Remove from the water and gently squeeze out any excess liquid. Place the gelatine in a small saucepan with 100ml of the whipped cream. Gently heat until completely dissolved. Remove from the heat.

Place the ricotta, mascarpone, sugar and vanilla extract in a food processor and blend until creamy. Transfer this to a large bowl. Add the gelatine mixture by straining it through a fine sieve. Fold in the remaining whipped cream. Crumble in the Oreo biscuits and mix gently. Spoon onto the biscuit base, cover and refrigerate for 24 hours.

Once chilled, transfer from the tin to a serving plate. Dust with cocoa powder or icing sugar to serve.

CHEF'S TIPS

+ Due to the high fat content in this cheesecake, it freezes well.
+ Allow the ricotta and mascarpone to come to room temperature before whisking.
+ For a seamless look and beautiful presentation, you can smooth the sides and top of the cheesecake with a knife dipped in hot water.

MINIATURE MERINGUE BITES

This is a variation on my traditional meringue roulade, which you will find on page 223. We were catering a large wedding and needed to come up with some ideas for sweet canapés, so we created these mini meringue roulades. They proved to be hugely popular!

prep: 15 minutes ✦ **cook**: 23 minutes ✦ **serves**: makes about 24

4 free-range egg whites

225g caster sugar

TO SERVE

200ml whipped cream

strawberries, raspberries or soft fruit of
  your choice

mint leaves to garnish

YOU WILL ALSO NEED

32 x 20cm Swiss roll tin

Preheat the oven to 165°C fan/185°C/gas mark 4.

Line the Swiss roll tin with tin foil and brush lightly with sunflower or vegetable oil, which won't affect the flavour. This prevents the meringue from sticking.

In a clean, dry bowl, beat the egg whites a little and then add the sugar and whisk until the mixture forms stiff peaks. Using a palette knife, gently spread out the meringue in the lined tin. It should be thick and quite bouncy.

Bake in the preheated oven for 23 minutes. Remove from the oven and set aside to cool.

With a pastry cutter (you can use any size, but a 4cm cutter should yield 24 bites), cut out miniature meringue rings and continue until you have used up all the meringue.

Spread whipped cream over half the meringue rings, reserving some to pipe on top later. You can add fresh fruit in the middle here too if you like. Place another ring on top and finish by piping a rosette of cream on top. Garnish with fresh mint leaves and a little fresh fruit if you like. Dredge with icing sugar to serve.

CRUSHED ORANGE AND ALMOND CAKE

———— ✦✦✦ ————

I saw a very similar recipe to this in a book published by the famous Books for Cooks in Notting Hill, London. I was there recently and the shelves were crammed floor to ceiling with so many gorgeous books. They also have a test kitchen and they have a wonderful motto: "Food here is not just something to be perused in books, it is something to be cooked, eaten and enjoyed."

prep: 70 minutes ✦ **cook**: 55 minutes ✦ **serves**: 14

FOR THE CAKE

2 oranges

250g caster sugar

250g unsalted butter, softened

300g ground almonds

1 tbsp baking powder

1 tbsp vanilla extract

6 organic or free-range eggs, separated

TO SERVE

icing sugar, to dust

crème fraîche or ice cream

YOU WILL ALSO NEED

23cm spring-form cake tin

Place the unpeeled, whole oranges in a saucepan and cover with cold water. Bring to the boil and reduce to simmer for 1 hour. Drain and then cut in quarters and remove the seeds and veins. Place in a food processor, while still warm, and blitz until the oranges form a smooth paste.

Preheat the oven to 165°C fan/185°C/gas mark 4. Prepare your tin by greasing it with butter and lining the base with non-stick parchment paper.

Add the sugar, butter, almonds, baking powder and vanilla extract to the orange mixture in the food processor and pulse gently until the mixture is combined. Continue to blitz the mixture as you add the six eggs, one at a time.

When everything is combined, pour the mixture into the tin and place on the middle rack of the oven for 55 minutes. Place an additional baking tray, filled with water, on the bottom rack of the oven. This will keep the cake beautifully moist.

Remove and leave to cool. Dust with icing sugar and serve with crème fraîche or ice cream.

———— ✦✦✦ ————

CHEF'S TIPS

+   You can replace the 2 oranges with 6 poached pears.
+   This cake is suitable for a coeliac, as the flour is replaced by the ground almonds.

THE BIG FEAST

CROWD PLEASERS

Black bean soup
Beef tomato salad with mustard dressing
Aidan Meyler's spicy chicken bake
Mascarpone and ricotta cheesecake

Wine suggestions
White: any big Chardonnay or an Antão Vaz from Portugal ✦ Rosé: a good dry rosé from Portugal or Germany

FINGERLICKING FOOD

Refried beans
Paul Arnold's pork souvlaki with tzatziki
BBQ spare ribs with mashed potatoes
Crushed orange and almond cake

Wine suggestions
White: a nice Chablis ✦ Red: a good full-bodied Italian red like a Touriga Nacional

SPICE IT UP

Spiced coleslaw
Asian chicken noodle soup
Beef Bourguignon
Miniature meringue bites

Wine suggestions
White: a dry white from the Loire Valley, such as a Chenin ✦ Red: a Syrah or Merlot from the south of France

THE MEDLEY
FUSION

◆◆◆

It's difficult to define the style of food we cook at Medley. My style is very eclectic, and my guests are always pleasantly surprised by how well the different flavours work together. Fusion cuisine combines elements of various culinary traditions while not fitting specifically into any one. You can mix it up a bit and combine French with Thai and Spanish with Italian. It is lovely to have Spanish tapas for your starter, Thai for your main course, and finish off with a typically French or Italian dessert. Alternatively you can have a selection of all the different cuisines on the table and just let your guests help themselves. The key is to keep it all very relaxed and to enjoy the sense of adventure.

GUACAMOLE

◆◆◆

Guacamole is an avocado-based dip that originated with the Aztecs in Mexico. In addition to its use in modern Mexican cooking it is very popular served as a dip or an accompaniment to grilled meat.

prep: 15 minutes ✦ **serves**: up to 10

½ small red onion, very finely chopped

½ tsp hot green chilli (serrano or jalapeño), trimmed, deseeded and very finely chopped

½ tsp hot red chilli (serrano or jalapeño), trimmed, deseeded and very finely chopped

1 medium vine-ripened tomato, deseeded and very finely chopped

2 garlic cloves, peeled and very finely chopped

bunch of fresh coriander leaves, chopped

3 medium ripe avocados

juice of ½ lime

½ tsp salt, or to taste

1 tbsp extra virgin olive oil

TO SERVE (OPTIONAL)

chopped onion

fresh coriander, chopped

cherry tomatoes, halved

crumbled feta or other cheese

Mix the finely chopped onion, chilli, tomato, garlic and coriander in a medium-sized bowl.

Cut into the avocados lengthwise, working your knife around the stone in the middle. Then twist the two halves in opposite directions to separate. Remove the stone and scoop out the flesh using a dessertspoon.

Place the avocado flesh in a bowl and pour over the lime juice (this prevents it from browning) and season with salt. Mash with a fork to a lumpy consistency. Add the remaining ingredients and mix well.

Immediately cover the guacamole with cling film, pushing the wrap down so that it is in direct contact with surface of the dip, to inhibit browning. Refrigerate for 1–2 hours to allow the flavours to develop and blend.

Serve with your choice of chopped onion, fresh coriander, halved cherry tomatoes or crumbled feta cheese.

◆◆◆

CHEF'S TIP

✦   The guacamole can also be loosened with crème fraîche. A lovely canapé idea is to make smoked salmon or Parma ham parcels with guacamole.

GAZPACHO

◆◆◆

Gazpacho is a chilled vegetable soup perfect for summer entertaining. Recipes for gazpacho tend to be very flexible; some include bread, others don't. In my recipe I have kept the ingredients very simple and accessible. In my view the bread is a must. It really does improve the texture and consistency. Rather than using raw tomatoes and peppers, I have roasted them with the garlic to improve the overall flavour. The important thing is not to be tempted to chill the gazpacho with ice cubes, as this dilutes the flavours.

prep: 30 minutes ◆ **chill**: 4 hours ◆ **serves**: 4

100g slightly stale crusty white bread

1 ripe red pepper

1 ripe green pepper

4 garlic cloves, roasted, peeled and crushed

100ml extra virgin olive oil

6 saffron stamens

1kg very ripe tomatoes, blanched, with skin and seeds removed

1 medium cucumber, peeled, cored and diced

2 tbsp sherry vinegar or red wine vinegar

½ tbsp balsamic vinegar

1 tsp salt

½ tsp freshly cracked black pepper

1 tsp sugar

½ tsp cayenne pepper

½ tsp smoked paprika

TO GARNISH, CHOICE OF

diced olives, prawns, strips of cucumber, hardboiled eggs or quail eggs (halved or quartered), sliced spring onion, croutons, fresh parsley or basil, celery, saffron stamens

Preheat oven to 200°C fan/220°C/gas mark 7

Soak the bread in cold water for 20 minutes and then squeeze out the water.

Cut the peppers in half and place on a roasting tray with the skin facing up. Place the garlic cloves in their skins on the roasting tray. Drizzle with the olive oil. Roast the peppers and garlic for 20 minutes. After the peppers have roasted, place them in ice-cold water for 3 minutes to help loosen the skin. Remove the skin, core and seeds from the peppers (see method p.229). Remove the skin from the garlic.

Soak the saffron in 50ml of water for 3 minutes. Then combine the roasted peppers, garlic and the remaining ingredients, including the pre-soaked bread, in a food processor. Blend until smooth or until it reaches your preferred texture. Cover and refrigerate for at least 4 hours to let the flavours infuse. Serve chilled, topped with croutons and garnishes of your choice.

◆◆◆

CHEF'S TIP

✦ You don't even have to pre-roast the garlic and peppers in this recipe.

✦ Using a sharp vegetable knife, cut a small 'X' on the base of each of the tomatoes before blanching. This will help with removing the skin afterwards.

TAPENADE

❖◆❖

Olive-based tapenades with anchovies are very Italian. I like to use tuna in my recipe, as it introduces an interesting dimension to the overall flavour. You can of course leave the tuna out if you prefer. I like to serve this alongside other dips and spreads such as olive oil, chicken liver pâté, tzatziki and hummus, with crusty bread. I regularly serve this as a tasting platter when I'm catering for large groups.

prep: 10 minutes ✦ **serves**: up to 20

200g salted anchovies, drained and rinsed in cold water

400g pitted black olives, chopped roughly

200g capers, drained and rinsed in cold water

200g canned tuna, drained

3 tbsp extra virgin olive oil

4 tbsp freshly squeezed lemon juice

sprig of fresh thyme, chopped

small bunch of fresh parsley, roughly chopped

2 garlic cloves, finely chopped

freshly cracked black pepper

2 tsp Dijon mustard

30ml brandy (optional)

After rinsing the anchovies, dry them on kitchen paper and roughly chop.

In a bowl, combine the olives, anchovies, capers and tuna. Add the olive oil, lemon juice, fresh herbs and garlic. Season with pepper and mustard (no need to add salt as the anchovies will be salty). Add a dash of brandy for a final flourish if you like. Any leftovers can be frozen.

Serve with crackers, crusty bread or crudités. Sprinkle with more fresh parsley.

❖◆❖

CHEF'S TIP

✦ Tapenade is a Provençal dish consisting of puréed or finely chopped olives, capers, anchovies and olive oil. The name comes from the Provençal word for capers, "tapenas".

CARROT AND CORIANDER SOUP

This soup is wholesome and nutritious and is very simple to make. To speed up the prep, use a food processor with a shredding attachment for the vegetables. Serve with Prue's treacle bread (recipe on page 193).

prep: 10 minutes ✦ **cook**: 25 minutes ✦ **serves**: up to 10

200g unsalted butter

1 tbsp olive oil

8 carrots, peeled and shredded (or grated)

1 onion, peeled and shredded (or grated)

1 parsnip, peeled and shredded (or grated)

2 large potatoes, peeled and shredded

1 tsp green Thai curry paste (see page 174 for recipe)

1 tsp curry powder

1.5 litres vegetable stock

salt and freshly cracked black pepper

125ml crème fraîche

1 bunch fresh coriander, stalks removed and finely chopped (optional)

Place a large saucepan over a medium heat and melt 150g butter with a dash of olive oil (this prevents the butter from burning) and sauté the carrots, onion, parsnip and potato for about 10 minutes until they become soft but not brown. Season with salt and pepper.

Add the green Thai curry paste and curry powder and mix well. Add the stock and season with salt and pepper. Bring to the boil and then reduce to simmer for about 15 minutes.

Remove from the heat and, using a hand blender, blend until smooth. Return to the pan and stir in the crème fraîche, fresh coriander (if using) and the additional 50g of butter to give it a smooth finish.

THAI FISH CAKES WITH CUCUMBER RELISH

This dish is one of the most popular canapés and starters I serve. The flavour balance is incredible. As with the Thai curry recipe on page 173, this one is all about the balance of the five fundamental tastes: hot (spicy), sour, sweet, salty and bitter. These fish cakes are bursting with flavour.

prep: 10 minutes ✦ **cook**: 8 minutes ✦ **makes**: about 35 (4–5 per person)

10 Kaffir lime leaves

2 tbsp fish sauce (nam pla)

1½ tbsp green or red curry paste

1 free-range egg

juice of ½ lime

2 tbsp sugar

1 tbsp chopped fresh coriander

600g white fish, such as cod or haddock, skin and bones removed

vegetable or sunflower oil for frying

TO SERVE

cucumber relish (see recipe on page 55)

To make the relish, see recipe on page 55.

To make the fishcakes, remove the tough veins from the Kaffir lime leaves and chop very finely with a knife. Add them to the bowl of a food processor with the rest of the ingredients (fish sauce, curry paste, egg, lime juice, sugar and coriander) except for the fresh fish and blend to a wet paste. Now add the fish and blitz for a further 30 seconds until well combined.

It is a good idea at this stage to fry off a little of the mixture in a frying pan and taste to see if you are happy with the flavour or if you need to add a little more lime juice, fish sauce or sugar etc. If you are happy with the flavour, remove the mixture from the bowl and refrigerate for approximately 1 hour to firm up.

Once firm, shape the mixture into small flat patties about 2cm thick and 5cm in diameter. You will find the mixture quite sticky, but if you wet your hands it's easier to work with. Store the patties in the fridge until you are ready to fry them.

Heat about 2cm sunflower or vegetable oil in a frying pan and, once hot, shallow fry the fishcakes for about 2 minutes on each side or until cooked through. You will need to fry them off in at least 2 batches, depending on the size of your pan. Once cooked, drain on kitchen paper and keep warm in the oven.

Serve the fish cakes immediately with the cucumber relish.

CHEF'S TIPS

✦ Don't cook the fish cakes too far in advance, as the texture will suffer. They don't take long to cook, so fry them off when everyone is sitting.

✦ Another lovely cheat's sauce for these is sweet chilli sauce mixed with sour cream and fresh coriander.

THAI PORK AND TURKEY SPRING ROLLS

◆◆◆

This Thai recipe for spring rolls is so simple to make and it can also be made as a vegetarian dish by simply omitting the meat. These rolls make great finger food for parties.

prep: 30 minutes ✦ **cook**: 3 minutes ✦ **makes**: about 40 spring rolls (10cm x 4cm)

FOR THE SPRING ROLLS

2 tbsp vegetable oil

1 onion, thinly sliced

1 large carrot, peeled and cut into julienne strips or coarsely grated

4 garlic cloves, crushed and finely chopped

2 stalks lemongrass, bruised and finely diced

2 chillies (red or green), finely chopped

5 tsp peeled and grated ginger

500g turkey mince

500g pork mince

100ml vegetable stock

2 tbsp soy sauce

1 tbsp fish sauce (nam pla)

1 tbsp toasted sesame oil

2 tsp rice vinegar

juice of ½ lime

2 tsp caster sugar

bunch of spring onions, finely sliced

1 x 198g tin sweetcorn

150g bean sprouts

4 tbsp fresh chopped coriander

40 squares of spring roll pastry, each 21.5cm x 21.5cm

In a frying pan, heat the vegetable oil. Lightly sauté the onion, carrot, garlic, lemongrass, fresh chilli and ginger for about 5 minutes until they are softened but not browned. Remove from the heat and allow to cool.

In a separate frying pan, heat some vegetable oil and add the turkey and pork mince. Cook for 10 minutes over a medium heat. Add the vegetable stock, soy sauce, fish sauce, sesame oil and rice vinegar and stir. Cook for a further 5 minutes over a high heat. At this point add the lime juice and sugar. Cook for a further 2 minutes. Check for seasoning. Then remove from the heat. If the mixture looks very lumpy you can transfer to a food processor and blitz for 30 seconds to break it up. It needs to be lump free to roll in the spring rolls.

Combine the pork and turkey mixture with the cooked vegetables and add the spring onion, bean sprouts, sweetcorn and coriander. Mix well. Check the seasoning. The weight of the mixture should be about 1.3kg.

Make sure the mixture is relatively dry before rolling. If necessary drain it in a colander.

Continued overleaf

1 tbsp rice wine vinegar

2 tbsp fish sauce (nam pla)

2 tbsp soy sauce

2 tbsp sweet chilli sauce

1 red chilli, deseeded and finely chopped

1 garlic clove, crushed

3 tbsp water

1 tbsp freshly squeezed lemon juice

To assemble the rolls, lay the spring roll wrappers on a clean, dry work surface. Place one tablespoon of filling on each wrapper (if making large spring rolls, use double the amount of filling). Spread the filling along the width of the spring roll wrapper towards the bottom of the wrapper (as illustrated opposite) — you'll want to leave about 1 inch from the corner of the wrapper closest to you, so you have room to roll it.

Then fold the corner of the wrapper up towards the middle and then fold in the sides of the wrapper and roll away from you. Secure the roll by using a damp pastry brush or by dipping the tip of your finger into some water and wetting the end, before giving it one last tight roll and sealing. The spring roll needs to be fairly tight. If it's too loose, it will disintegrate when frying.

Continue until you have used up all the spring roll wrappers.

To cook the spring rolls, shallow fry them in batches in vegetable oil for about 3 minutes or until golden brown. Drain on kitchen paper before serving.

To make the dipping sauce, simply combine all the ingredients in a bowl and mix well.

CHEF'S TIP

+ You will find the spring roll pastry in any good Asian food store.

Sweet Chilli Jam

Tomato Salsa

RED-HOT TOMATO AND PEPPER RELISH

◆◆◆

Chutneys and relishes are made from a combination of fruit, vegetables, vinegar, sugar, spices and salt. They're a wonderful way to use up vegetables that have been sitting around. The flavour of a relish or chutney will improve with time, and ideally they should be left to mature in a cool dark place for about a month before consumption. But they can of course be used immediately too. Bear in mind that chutneys and relishes can taste sharp and highly spiced when first made, and that they mellow with time.

prep: 15 minutes ◆ **cook**: 45 minutes

1 tbsp yellow mustard seeds, toasted and crushed

1 tbsp black mustard seeds, toasted and crushed

2 tsp celery seeds, toasted and crushed

2 tbsp coriander seeds, toasted and crushed

1.4kg ripe tomatoes, peeled, deseeded and chopped (alternatively you can use 3 x 400g tins of chopped tomatoes)

1 onion, peeled and finely chopped

200g red peppers, trimmed, deseeded and roughly chopped

250g yellow peppers, trimmed, deseeded and roughly chopped

3 fresh chillies, finely chopped (mixture of green and red)

100g caster sugar

100g brown sugar

200ml red wine vinegar

1 tbsp smoked paprika

salt and freshly cracked black pepper

To toast the spices, simply place a pan over a medium heat, and once hot, add the spices to the dry pan and let them toast until they become fragrant. This little trick really boosts the flavour of spices.

Put the tomatoes, onions, peppers and chillies in a large saucepan, cover and cook over a low heat for 12 minutes, stirring occasionally. Add the sugar and vinegar and slowly bring to the boil, stirring occasionally until the sugar has dissolved completely.

Add the toasted and crushed mustard seeds, celery seeds, coriander seeds, paprika, salt and pepper and stir well. Increase the heat and cook the mixture uncovered for 30 minutes. This will allow some of the liquid to evaporate and will produce a thick but moist consistency. Stir frequently. Then remove from the heat and allow to cool.

Spoon the relish into warm sterilised Kilner jars (see below). Cover and seal. Store in a cool, dark cupboard for up to 2 months.

---◆◆◆---

CHEF'S TIP

✦ To sterilise a Kilner or jam jar, remove the lids or rubber seals from the jars and place to one side. Place the jars in a saucepan and fill with water until the jars are covered. Bring to the boil and keep at the maximum temperature for 10–12 minutes. Turn off the heat and cover the pan to keep the jars warm until you are ready to fill them. If you are using a Kilner-style jar, place the rubber seals in a small pan and cover with about 10cm of water. Simmer at 85°C for 10–12 minutes and then turn off the heat and cover the pan until you are ready to seal the jars.

SWEET CHILLI AND RED PEPPER JAM

I have been making this jam for years. It's always a favourite and works well with a variety of dishes. Most recently I served it with the slow-roast belly of pork (see recipe on page 105). It also works well with cold meats and as something to spice up a traditional cooked breakfast.

prep: 10 minutes ✦ **cook**: 1 hour 10 minutes ✦ **makes**: about 1.75kg (3½ x 500g Kilner jars)

8 red peppers, trimmed, deseeded and roughly chopped

6 red chillies, finely chopped

5cm fresh ginger, peeled and finely chopped or grated

6 garlic cloves, peeled and finely chopped

400g cherry tomatoes (fresh or tinned)

250ml red wine vinegar

700g caster sugar

YOU WILL ALSO NEED

a selection of jam jars or Kilner jars

Turn to page 165 for directions on how to sterilise your jars.

Place the red peppers, chilli, ginger and garlic into a food processor. You can add the seeds from the fresh chillies, too, if you like a bit of heat. Blitz until finely chopped.

Transfer the mixture to a heavy-bottomed saucepan with the tomatoes, vinegar and sugar. Bring to the boil over a high heat. After 5 minutes, remove any surface residue or scum and reduce the heat to medium. Let the mixture bubble away gently for 60 minutes, uncovered, stirring occasionally.

Once the mixture is reduced by about 40 per cent, remove from the heat. The consistency should be thick and syrupy. You can cook for longer if you want a thicker consistency. The longer you cook the mixture the more it will reduce and thicken, and the taste and colour will intensify.

Cool and transfer the jam to sterilised Kilner jars or glass jam jars. Store in a cool, dry place.

CHEF'S TIP

✦ This jam will keep for up to 2 months. Once opened, store in the fridge and use within 2 weeks. It's also a lovely idea to give this jam as a gift in a nicely presented Kilner jar.

CHICKEN SATAY

◆◆◆

My friend Ruth introduced me to this dish and to the wonderful flavours of Thai food, as she has done with so many other flavours from around the world. This takes no time to prepare and the results are incredibly tasty.

prep: 10 minutes ◆ **marinate**: 30 minutes or overnight ◆ **cook**: 3–4 minutes ◆ **serves**: 8

4 skinless, boneless chicken breasts, sliced into strips

FOR THE MARINADE

2 tbsp clear honey

2 tbsp soy sauce

2 tbsp fish sauce (nam pla)

a few drops Tabasco

2 garlic cloves, crushed

5cm piece fresh ginger root, grated

1 stalk of lemongrass, peeled, bruised and finely chopped

FOR THE SPICY PEANUT SAUCE

2 garlic cloves, crushed

2 small chilli peppers, finely diced

1 tbsp hot chilli paste/sauce, or more if you like

juice of ½ lime, or more if you like

2 tbsp grated fresh ginger

1½–2 tbsp caster sugar, or more if you like (this is not absolutely necessary)

2 tbsp dark soy sauce

2 tbsp Worcestershire sauce

1 tbsp toasted sesame oil

3 tbsp coconut milk

1 tbsp chopped fresh coriander leaves

1 jar smooth peanut butter (normally 510g)

100ml boiling water, if required

Begin by preparing the marinade. Simply put all the ingredients in a bowl and whisk them until combined (or you can put them in a large ziplock bag and give it a shake). Place the chicken pieces in the marinade, making sure they are well coated, and cover the bowl (or seal the bag) and set aside for at least 30 minutes. Overnight would be better.

In the meantime, prepare the peanut sauce dressing by blending all the ingredients in a food processor, with the exception of the peanut butter and boiling water. This will ensure that the flavour is evenly distributed. Then add the peanut butter to the mixture in the food processor and whizz for 30 seconds. The mixture needs to be smooth and should have the consistency of heavy cream. If it is too thick, drizzle in some hot water, as this will loosen it. If it becomes too thin, add more peanut butter.

Remove the chicken strips from the marinade, drain and pat dry with kitchen towel. Grill them on a hot griddle pan or a non-stick frying pan for about 2–3 minutes on each side. Serve on warm plates with the peanut sauce on the side.

◆◆◆

CHEF'S TIPS

◆ This chicken satay is lovely served as a canapé or a starter. If you don't use all of the peanut sauce, pour it back into the tub and store in the fridge for up to 1 week.

◆ Another lovely way to serve this dish is to completely coat the grilled chicken strips in the peanut sauce and serve on a bed of noodles also coated with the peanut sauce.

SEAFOOD PAELLA

◆◆◆

This is regarded by the Spanish as a Valencian dish. It can be made with seafood, chicken, rabbit or vegetables. According to Valencian tradition, paella is cooked by men over an open fire fuelled by orange and pine branches along with pine cones. This produces an aromatic smoke that infuses the paella. My version uses spice to make it beautifully fragrant.

prep: 20 minutes ✦ **cook**: 30 minutes ✦ **serves**: 4–6

2 medium onions, sliced

1 red pepper, trimmed, deseeded and cut into thin strips

1 green pepper, trimmed, deseeded and cut into thin strips

4 garlic cloves, peeled and chopped

150ml extra virgin olive oil

2 tsp turmeric

1½ tsp sweet pimentón or paprika

1½ tsp chilli powder

salt and freshly cracked black pepper

150g monkfish cut into chunks

150g medium uncooked prawns, peeled and deveined

150g squid, body and tentacles only, cleaned and cut into 2cm pieces, flesh scored

1 tbsp coarse sea salt

500g bomba rice (or basmati or long-grain), unrinsed

2 litres hot fish stock (chicken or vegetable are fine too)

pinch of saffron (infused in the stock)

225g mussels, scrubbed and debearded

225g clams

TO SERVE

2 lemons, cut into wedges

fresh flat leaf parsley, to garnish

Preheat the oven to 200°C fan/220°C/gas mark 7.

Place the onion, peppers and garlic in a medium-sized roasting dish and drizzle over a generous amount of olive oil. Roast in the oven for 15 minutes. Remove the skin from the peppers (see method on page 229).

Heat 2 tablespoons of olive oil in a deep frying pan or paella dish over a medium heat. Add the roasted vegetables, turmeric, pimentón (or paprika), chilli, salt and pepper and mix well.

Add the monkfish, prawns, squid, and sea salt. Add a little more oil if the mixture seems too dry. Increase the heat to medium and sauté for 5 minutes. Add the rice and stir gently.

Pour in three-quarters of the stock. Increase the heat to high and bring to a boil. Reduce to simmer and cook for 10–15 minutes or until the rice is cooked. Add more stock if necessary. Don't stir the paella too much as you don't want the ingredients to go mushy.

Add the mussels and clams. Cook for a further 5 minutes. Remove from the heat and add the lemon juice and the remaining stock. Fork through gently, cover and leave to stand for 5 minutes before serving.

Discard any unopened clams or mussels. Serve the paella with lemon wedges on the side and a sprinkle of fresh parsley on top.

◆◆◆

CHEF'S TIPS

+ After roasting the peppers, remove from the hot oven and immediately submerge in iced water. This will help to remove the roasted skin; it will peel straight off.

+ A great way to tenderise squid is to criss-cross the flesh with a sharp knife and soak it overnight in 500ml milk and 1 tsp bicarbonate of soda. Just before cooking the paella, drain the squid, pat dry with kitchen paper and slice into rings or strips.

FRAGRANT THAI CHICKEN CURRY

◆◆◆

Thai cuisine places emphasis on light dishes with strong aromatic components. Balance, detail and variety are very important in Thai cooking, and it is known for balancing the five fundamental tastes: hot (spicy), sour, sweet, salty, and bitter.

prep: 10 minutes ✦ **cook**: 40–45 minutes ✦ **serves**: 6

FOR THE STOCK

1.5 litres chicken stock

5 cardamom pods, toasted until fragrant

2 cinnamon sticks

4 garlic cloves, peeled and roughly chopped

10 Kaffir lime leaves, deveined and sliced into thin strips

2 stalks of lemongrass, bruised and finely chopped

5cm piece of fresh ginger, peeled and roughly chopped

2 small chilli peppers, roughly chopped in 3

FOR THE CURRY

1 tbsp Thai curry paste (you can use green or red – see recipe overleaf)

5 baby potatoes, cut in half

6 free-range chicken breasts, trimmed and diced into 2cm pieces

1 large onion, diced

1 red pepper, trimmed, deseeded and cut into chunks

1 green pepper, deseeded and cut into chunks

1 courgette, cut into chunks

2 tbsp fish sauce (nam pla)

juice of 1 fresh lime

To prepare the stock, bring 1.5 litres of chicken stock to the boil in a stockpot or large saucepan. Then add the cardamom pods, cinnamon sticks, garlic, Kaffir lime leaves, lemongrass, ginger and chilli pepper. Bring to the boil and then simmer for 20 minutes. Remove from the heat. Once cool, pass through a sieve. Retain the liquid and discard the remaining ingredients.

To make the curry, pour 1 tablespoon of stock into a large heavy-based pan (with a lid) and heat gently over a medium heat. Add the curry paste and cook for a few minutes until it has combined with the stock. Taste and add more paste if desired, depending on how hot you like your curry. Add the remaining stock and potato chunks. Bring to the boil. Reduce the heat and simmer for 15 minutes. Add the chicken pieces and cook for a further 15 minutes or until the chicken is tender and cooked through. Add the onions, peppers and courgette. Simmer until the vegetables are cooked through but still holding their shape. This should take about 5–10 minutes.

Add the fish sauce, lime juice, sugar and coconut milk and cook for a further 5 minutes over a low heat. Do not let the temperature become too hot or the sauce will split. Taste and add more sugar or lime juice if you feel it needs it.

Serve with fluffy steamed rice and garnish with fresh coriander leaves and crushed peanuts.

1 tbsp caster sugar

200ml coconut milk

TO SERVE

steamed rice

roasted peanuts, roughly crushed

fresh coriander leaves, roughly chopped

FOR THE CURRY PASTE

4 medium green chillies, deseeded and
   roughly chopped

3 shallots, roughly chopped

5cm piece fresh ginger, peeled and grated

3 garlic cloves, crushed

small bunch of fresh coriander, stalks and
   leaves

2 lemongrass stalks, bruised and finely
   chopped

zest and juice of 1 lime

8 Kaffir lime leaves, torn into pieces

2.5cm piece galangal (if available), peeled
   and chopped

1 tbsp coriander seeds, crushed

1 tsp ground cumin

1 tsp black peppercorns, crushed

2 tsp Thai fish sauce (or light soy sauce for
   a vegetarian version)

3 tbsp sunflower oil

TO MAKE YOUR OWN CURRY PASTE

Place all the ingredients in a food processor and blitz to a smooth
paste. It will keep in an airtight jar in the fridge for up to 2 weeks.
Or you can freeze it in ice cube trays, which provides the perfect
portion size of paste for a curry.

WHAT'S THE DIFFERENCE BETWEEN RED AND GREEN CURRIES?

Traditionally all Thai curries were made with the same ingredients
except for one thing — the chillies. Red curry was made with red
chillies, while green curry was made with green chillies and yellow
curry was made with yellow chillies. In Thailand these chillies
have slightly different flavour characteristics.

Green curry has a more vibrant green these days, with the addition
of fresh coriander, Kaffir lime leaves and Thai basil. Red curry
has more or less remained the same, with traditional Thai chefs
adding up to 20 red chillies to make it very red and fiery hot.
However, some modern chefs prefer to use fewer chillies and
instead use chilli powder, which enhances the red colour of this
curry as well as giving it greater depth of flavour.

CHEF'S TIPS

+ To roast spices, simply place a pan over a medium heat, and
   once hot, add the fresh spices to the dry pan and let them roast
   until they release their wonderful smell and become fragrant.
   This little trick really boosts the flavour of fresh spices.

+ If you can't get Kaffir lime leaves, use the grated zest of 1
   additional lime.

HERBES
DE
PROVENCE
50g → 3€
100g → 5€

Herbes de Provence

Herbes de Provence

...es de Provence

...Provence

Caramelle
50g → 4€
100g → 7€

Muscade
3€ les 5g

LAMB TAGINE

❖❖❖

Tagine is a traditional casserole-style dish from Morocco and can be prepared well in advance. The combination of aromatic spices, fruits and succulent lamb produces an exquisite dish bursting with flavour.

prep: 30 minutes ✦ **marinate**: overnight ✦ **cook**: 2–2½ hours ✦ **serves**: 4–8

FOR THE SPICE MIX

1 tsp cayenne pepper

1 tsp ground turmeric

2 tsp freshly cracked black pepper

1½ tbsp paprika

1½ tbsp ground ginger

1 tsp coriander seeds, roasted and crushed

2 tbsp ground cinnamon

FOR THE TAGINE

1 x shoulder of lamb, trimmed and cut into
    5cm chunks (about 1kg in total)

2 tbsp olive oil

2 tbsp sunflower oil or vegetable oil

2 large onions, peeled and grated

3 garlic cloves, crushed

570ml tomato juice

2 x 400g tins chopped tomatoes

115g dried apricots, cut in half

55g dates, cut in half

55g raisins or sultanas

100g flaked almonds, lightly toasted

1 tsp saffron threads, soaked in cold water

600ml lamb stock (chicken is fine too)

1 tbsp clear honey

2 tbsp chopped fresh coriander

2 tbsp chopped fresh flat leaf parsley

Place the spice mix ingredients into a small bowl and mix to combine.

Place the lamb chunks in a large bowl and toss together with half of the spice mix. Cover and leave overnight in the fridge.

Heat 1 tablespoon olive oil and 1 tablespoon sunflower or vegetable oil in a large casserole pot (with a lid). Add the grated onion and the remaining spice mix and cook over a gentle heat for 10 minutes so that the onions are soft but not coloured. Add the crushed garlic for the final 3 minutes.

In a separate frying pan, heat the remaining oil and brown the cubes of lamb on all sides. Then add the browned meat to the casserole dish. Deglaze the frying pan with 150ml tomato juice and add these juices to the casserole.

Preheat the oven to 130° fan/150°C/gas mark 2.

Add the remaining tomato juice, chopped tomatoes, apricots, dates, raisins or sultanas, half the flaked almonds, saffron, lamb stock and honey to the casserole dish and stir well. Bring to the boil, cover with a fitted lid and place in the oven. Cook for 2–2½ hours, or until the meat is meltingly tender.

When it comes out of the oven, put the lamb in a traditional clay tagine pot or in a large serving dish and sprinkle over the chopped herbs and the remaining toasted flaked almonds.

Serve with rice or couscous.

❖❖❖

CHEF'S TIP

✦   If you prefer, you can just place all the ingredients into a large casserole dish and stick it in the oven. This method avoids browning the lamb separately, which takes time and effort.

THAI STIR-FRIED BEEF WITH OYSTER SAUCE

◆◆◆

This is such a simple recipe and it's so quick to prepare. It is without a doubt one of the most popular dishes we serve in Medley. Why not try this as one of the dishes if you are doing a themed Thai evening? It's a good idea to have the kitchen window open while you fry the vegetables. The combination of chilli and garlic can produce very strong aromas that can irritate your eyes and throat. It's worth it, though!

prep: 10 minutes ◆ **marinate**: 30 minutes or up to 1 hour ◆ **cook**: 10 minutes ◆ **serves**: 6

FOR THE STIR-FRY

2 tbsp soy sauce

1 tbsp cornflour

500g fillet steak (you can also use rump), cut into thin strips

3 tbsp vegetable oil

1 tbsp chopped garlic

1 tbsp chopped or grated fresh ginger root

1 green pepper, trimmed, deseeded and cut into strips (optional)

1 red pepper, trimmed, deseeded and cut into strips (optional)

1 yellow pepper, trimmed, deseeded and cut into strips (optional)

1 fresh red chilli, seeds removed and cut into thin strips

1 fresh green chilli, seeds removed and cut into thin strips

250g mixed mushrooms

FOR THE OYSTER SAUCE

3 tbsp oyster sauce

2 tsp granulated sugar

2 tsp fish sauce

juice of ½ lime

1 tsbsp water

4 spring onions, cut into short lengths

freshly cracked black pepper

Mix together the soy sauce and cornflour. Add the steak and coat well. Leave to marinate at room temperature for 30 minutes or up to 1 hour.

Heat 1 tablespoon of oil in a wok. Add the garlic, ginger, peppers (if using) and chilli and fry for 1–2 minutes, until softened but not brown.

Add the steak to the wok. Stir-fry for about 4 minutes or until the meat is browned and tender. Remove from the heat and cover to keep warm.

Heat the remaining oil in a separate pan. Add the mushrooms. Stir-fry until golden brown. Add the sautéed mushrooms to the stir-fry in the wok.

In a separate small pan, combine the oyster sauce, sugar, fish sauce, lime juice, water and spring onions. Mix well and add pepper to taste, if required. Cook for 2 minutes.

Pour the oyster sauce mixture over the stir-fry and mix well. You can also give it one last blast of heat in your wok after you've added all the ingredients.

Serve immediately with fluffy steamed rice.

◆

CHEF'S TIP

◆ For lovely fragrant rice, add a few cardamom pods, ½ stalk of bruised lemongrass and ½ tsp ground turmeric to the cooking water.

COCONUT RICE PUDDING

This creamy coconut milk rice pudding is a warm and comforting treat that's infused with lemongrass and cinnamon. It works beautifully with many of the other puddings featured in this book. I know that people generally don't like rice pudding, but this recipe has always been a crowd pleaser.

prep: 5 minutes ✦ **cook**: 1½ hours ✦ **serves**: 6–8

200g short grain pudding rice

180g caster sugar

½ tsp vanilla essence

1 tsp ground cinnamon

3 stalks of lemongrass, bruised

900ml milk

400ml coconut milk

TO SERVE

2 tbsp desiccated coconut, roasted

Wash the rice and drain well. Soak the rice, sugar, vanilla, cinnamon, lemongrass, milk and coconut milk in an ovenproof dish or clay pot for 15 minutes, stirring occasionally.

Preheat the oven to 150°C fan/170°C/gas mark 3.

Cover the mixture and cook in the low oven for 1½ hours. Remove from the oven and stir the pudding. Then sprinkle over the desiccated coconut (or slivers of fresh coconut) before serving.

Serve immediately.

BROWN BREAD ICE CREAM

━━━━━ ◆◆◆ ━━━━━

The first time I had brown bread ice cream was in the early nineties, when my sister Emma made it after completing a cookery course. Many years later I was asked by Brennan's Bread to create an ice cream that contained wholewheat bread to the menu. With anything sweet, it's important to get a good balance of flavour without having it too sweet. This recipe works extraordinarily well. If it's an adult–only treat, add two extra tablespoons of booze.

prep: 30 minutes ◆ **freeze**: overnight ◆ **serves**: 6–8

120g wholewheat bread

150g muscovado sugar

200ml single cream

100ml full-fat milk

2 tsp vanilla extract

2 organic or free-range egg yolks

2 organic or free-range eggs

1 tbsp rum, Tia Maria or coffee liqueur (3 for adults)

300ml double cream

Preheat the oven to 160°C fan/180°C/gas mark 4.

In a food processor, blend the bread to make crumbs. Add 100g sugar and mix well. Line a baking tray with greaseproof paper and spread the crumbs out in an even layer. Bake for 10 minutes or until golden brown. Be careful not to let them burn. Remove from the oven, allow to cool and blitz in the food processor once again.

In a saucepan, combine the single cream, milk and vanilla extract. Gently bring to a simmer. Remove from the heat and allow to cool while the flavours infuse.

In a bowl, whisk the egg yolks, eggs and remaining sugar until pale and fluffy. Transfer to a saucepan to make the custard by adding the infused cream mixture slowly over a gentle heat. Keep stirring over a low heat for about 5 minutes or until the mixture thickens slightly. Remove from the heat and add the rum, Tia Maria or coffee liqueur. Transfer to a clean bowl and allow to cool.

Whisk the double cream in a separate bowl and then add to the custard. Mix in the breadcrumbs.

Pour the ice cream mixture into a plastic container and place in the freezer for two hours. Remove from the freezer, and give it a good mix to break the mixture up. The breadcrumbs will have fallen to the bottom, so make sure to combine them back into the body of the mixture. Then return to the freezer for a further hour. Remove and repeat the process as above. Now leave the ice cream in the freezer for another 2 hours or until it has just about set but is not yet completely hard. Remove and beat well one last time, cover with cling film and then return to the freezer overnight or until you are ready to serve.

Transfer from the freezer to the fridge 20 minutes before serving, to soften.

MICHAEL KELLY'S GRAPEFRUIT TARRAGON LAYER CAKE

❖❖❖

My friend Mike, who lives in San Francisco, would love to open his own restaurant or bistro. He is a consummate foodie. When I asked if he would like to contribute to this book, he certainly pulled out all the stops. His friends were treated to many prototypes before he came up with this remarkable recipe. He says, "I will admit there are a few component parts to this cake, but it is not as difficult to make as it sounds! The beauty is that the cream filling, syrup and cake can each be made a day in advance and stored in the fridge until you're ready to complete the icing and serve. The grapefruit syrup is a nice addition, but it is optional." This is my interpretation of Michael's recipe.

prep: up to 1 hour ✦ **chill**: 2–3 hours ✦ **cook**: up to 2 hours ✦ **serves**: 10–12

FOR THE GRAPEFRUIT CREAM FILLING

310ml grapefruit juice

6 large free-range eggs

2 large free-range egg yolks

340g caster sugar

large pinch salt

zest ½ grapefruit, organic if possible

450g unsalted butter, softened but still cool

FOR THE GRAPEFRUIT SYRUP (OPTIONAL)

75g caster sugar

60ml freshly squeezed grapefruit juice

2 tbsp freshly squeezed lemon juice

FOR THE GRAPEFRUIT TARRAGON CAKE

1 grapefruit

300g butter, cubed

3 tbsp chopped fresh tarragon

210g self-raising flour

150g plain flour

3 tsp baking powder

300g light muscovado sugar

300g caster sugar

6 large free-range eggs, separated

To make the grapefruit cream filling, fill a medium saucepan one-third full with water, place over a medium heat and bring to a simmer. Into a heatproof or stainless steel bowl, add the grapefruit juice, whole eggs, egg yolks, sugar and salt. Mix the ingredients until well combined. Then rest the bowl in the saucepan, making sure it doesn't touch the water. Whisk continuously until the mixture thickens, lightens and registers 82°C on a cook's thermometer. This will take approximately 15–18 minutes. Do not stop whisking the mixture while it is over the water, as this can cause the yolks to cook and create lumps in the mixture. Remove the bowl from the saucepan and add the grapefruit zest to the mixture. Allow to cool to 60°C.

While the mixture is cooling, cut the cool butter into 2cm cubes. When the mixture reaches 60°C, add the butter one piece at a time. Using a hand blender, blend until each cube is incorporated before adding the next piece of butter. The mixture will deflate during the cooling process and will become pale yellow and thick. Cover and chill completely in the refrigerator until ready to use, about 2–3 hours depending on your refrigerator.

To make the grapefruit syrup, combine all the ingredients in a small saucepan and place over a medium heat. Stirring constantly, bring to the boil and then remove from the heat and cover until needed (or refrigerate if making in advance). Strain the syrup. If it has been refrigerated, warm the syrup again before using.

Preheat the oven to 160°C fan/180°C/gas mark 4.

Continued overleaf

100ml buttermilk

2 tsp bicarbonate soda (baking soda)

125ml tepid water

½ tbsp vanilla extract

FOR THE GRAPEFRUIT ICING

125g butter, softened

200g icing sugar, sifted

zest of 1 grapefruit

1 tbsp milk

1 tsp vanilla extract

YOU WILL ALSO NEED

2 x 23cm cake tins

cook's thermometer

To make the grapefruit tarragon cake, grease and flour two 23cm cake tins. Line the bottoms with parchment paper and grease the sides with butter.

Steam the grapefruit for 1 hour. Cut off the ends and remove the central pith, veins and pips. Cut into 4 segments. While the fruit is still warm blitz with the butter and chopped tarragon in a food processor. Now sieve all of the following dry ingredients into a bowl: self-raising flour, plain flour, baking powder, muscovado sugar and caster sugar. In a separate bowl quickly mix the egg yolks. And in another bowl whisk the egg whites until they form stiff peaks. Combine the grapefruit and butter and tarragon mixture with the sieved dry ingredients and add the egg yolks and buttermilk. Stir to make sure the mixture is fully combined. In another bowl mix the bicarbonate of soda with the tepid water. This will start to froth and foam within 30 seconds. Immediately pour this in to the batter mix. Finally, fold in the egg whites with a metal spoon, divide the batter between the two cake tins and transfer to the preheated oven immediately.

Bake the cakes on the middle shelf of the oven, until a skewer comes out clean from the centre of each cake. This will take approximately 1 hour 40 minutes. Rotate the tins 180° halfway through baking. Remove the cakes from the oven and, using a skewer, poke holes all over the top of the cakes, going through to the pan. Brush the grapefruit syrup liberally over the cakes, letting the syrup soak into the cake before re-applying. You should use about 120ml of the syrup between the two cakes. Allow the cakes to cool for 10 minutes and then remove them from their tins and let them cool completely on wire racks for about 2–3 hours.

To assemble, first line the edges of a cake platter with strips of parchment paper to keep the plate clean while assembling. Cut each cake horizontally into two even layers and place the bottom layer of one cake on the platter. Spread 235ml of the grapefruit cream evenly on the cake, leaving a 1.5cm border around the edge. Carefully place the other half of the cake on top of the filling. Spread another 235ml of the cream on top and repeat with the remaining layers. Smooth any filling that leaked out the sides with a spatula. Cover with plastic wrap and place in the refrigerator until ready to ice (you can do everything up to this point up to a day in advance).

To make the grapefruit icing put the butter into a large bowl and beat with an electric hand-mixer until light and fluffy. Sieve in the icing sugar and work into the butter, starting slowly at first and then more vigorously until all the sugar is combined. Add in the grapefruit zest, milk and vanilla extract and beat until smooth and creamy. If the mixture is too firm, simply add another tablespoon of milk. Spread the icing evenly over the top of the cake and remove the parchment from the cake platter. Chill in the refrigerator if not serving immediately.

CHEF'S TIP

+ Please follow the instructions to the letter and use a thermometer.

THE MEDLEY FUSION

TERRIFIC THAI

Thai pork and turkey spring rolls
Fragrant Thai chicken curry
Coconut rice pudding

Wine suggestions
White: a good quality Pinot blanc or a dry German Riesling

SPANISH SENSATION

Gazpacho
Seafood paella
Michael Kelly's grapefruit tarragon layer cake

Wine suggestions
White: an Albarino from Rias Baixas ✦ *Red: a low-alcohol, low-tannin Spanish Garnacha*

GLOBAL GOURMET

Thai fish cakes with cucumber relish
Lamb tagine
Brown bread ice cream

Wine suggestions
White: a Grüner Veltliner from Austria ✦ *Red: a nice Côtes du Rhône or a Bordeaux-style Cabernet*

BRUNCH AND LONG
LAZY LUNCH

I love entertaining on Sundays and sometimes even Friday afternoons if work permits. My schedule generally means that I am working on Friday and Saturday nights, so I really look forward to Sunday. There's nothing nicer than knowing I have friends coming over to share a long, lazy Sunday – that may well spill into the early hours. With this in mind, it's easy-to-prepare comfort food that fits the bill perfectly for these occasions. Most of the recipes in this chapter can be prepared in advance. So all you have to do is set the table, chill the wine and gently warm the food. Bliss!

PRUE'S TREACLE BREAD

This is my mum's recipe and she has been making it for years. When we were growing up, Mum was always great with breads. She made white yeast bread rolls and we would have ox tongue sandwiches. I remember going into the kitchen every lunchtime during the summer months and on the back of the AGA there always sat a baking tray wrapped in black bin liners, to help prove the bread. This bread goes really well with many of the dishes in this book.

prep: 10 minutes ✦ **cook**: 40–45 minutes ✦ **serves**: 10–15

500g plain flour

50g wholewheat flour

1 heaped tsp baking powder

1 heaped tsp bread soda

1 tsp caster sugar

350ml buttermilk

1 tbsp treacle

Preheat the oven to 180°C fan/200°C/gas mark 6.

Mix all the dry ingredients in a mixing bowl and make a well in the centre.

In a separate bowl, mix the buttermilk and treacle together until well combined. Then add to the dry mixture. Mix in concentric circles using a knife until all the flour and liquid are combined. The dough should be soft but not too sticky at this stage. It's important that the mix is not too wet. If it is very wet, simply sprinkle in an additional tablespoon of flour and combine.

Turn the mixture out onto a floured surface. Flour your hands and knead for a couple of minutes. If your hands get sticky, dust them with flour again. Shape the dough into an oval or round (about 7–8cm high) and, using a sharp knife, slash a large X into the top of the dough. You could also use a loaf tin if you prefer.

Place on a floured baking tray and bake in the oven for 40–45 minutes. Check if the bread is done by tapping the base; it should sound hollow. If it doesn't, pop it back in the oven for a further 5 minutes.

Leave to cool on a wire rack.

MUSHROOMS ON TOAST

I have to say that this is one of my favourite snacks. It's quick and tasty and it was a staple in our house when I was growing up. This recipe is certainly one of my mum's greatest achievements, apart from rearing her brood of children, of course!

prep: 5 minutes ✦ **cook**: 12 minutes ✦ **serves**: 4

40g butter

400g button mushrooms, roughly chopped

1 small onion, finely diced

2 cloves garlic, crushed

3 tsp chopped fresh thyme

salt and freshly cracked black pepper

40g plain flour

300ml milk

100ml cream

TO SERVE

4 slices of ciabatta, toasted

chopped fresh parsley (optional)

Place a heavy-bottomed pan over a medium heat and melt the butter. Once the butter is foaming, add the mushrooms, onion, garlic and thyme. Season with salt and pepper and gently sauté until the mushrooms are softened but not browned. This should take about 4 minutes.

Stir in the flour and cook for 1 minute. Add the milk and bring to the boil. Reduce the heat and simmer for 6 minutes to cook out the flour. Then stir in the cream. Taste and season with salt and pepper to taste. Cook for a further minute.

Serve immediately on freshly toasted rustic bread and sprinkle over some chopped fresh parsley if you like.

CHEF'S TIP
✦ Add more cream if you need to loosen the mixture.

EGGS BENEDICT

◆◆◆

In Darina Allen's words, "Hollandaise is the mother of all the warm emulsion sauces." In appearance it should be light yellow and opaque, and smooth and creamy in texture. The flavour is rich and buttery, with a mild tang added by an acidic component such as lemon juice. This is one of my favourite breakfast treats.

prep: 10 minutes ◆ **cook**: 15 minutes ◆ **serves**: 4

FOR THE HOLLANDAISE SAUCE

4 large free-range egg yolks

2 tsp lemon juice

120g butter, melted

pinch of cayenne pepper

salt and freshly cracked black pepper

FOR THE POACHED EGGS

2 tbsp freshly squeezed lemon juice

1 tsp salt

8 large free-range eggs

TO SERVE

8 slices bacon (optional)

4 bagels or English muffins, split in half
  and lightly toasted

3 tbsp chopped fresh chives

Begin by making the hollandaise sauce. Blend the egg yolks and lemon juice in a blender until smooth and frothy, about 10 seconds. With the blender running, very slowly drizzle in half the melted butter until the mixture is quite thick. This will take about 1½ minutes. Transfer the mixture to a bain-marie set over a low to medium heat on the hob. Begin to cook the mixture slowly and add the remaining butter. Continue to cook until the sauce thickens to a consistency that will coat the back of a spoon. Stir in the cayenne pepper and season with salt and pepper, to taste. Turn the heat under the bain-marie to the very lowest setting and allow the hollandaise to sit in the bowl to keep warm. Do not attempt to heat it any more than this before serving as it may split.

Next, fry the bacon over a medium heat until well-browned on each side. When cooked, transfer to a plate lined with kitchen paper, and cover with foil to keep warm.

While the bacon is cooking, fill a saucepan nearly to the brim with water. Add the lemon juice and a teaspoon of salt and bring to a gentle simmer over a medium heat. When the water comes to a simmer crack an egg into a cup and carefully slide it into the hot poaching liquid. Quickly repeat with the remaining eggs. Using a slotted spoon carefully corral the white of each egg around its yolk. Poach the eggs, turning them periodically with a slotted spoon, until the whites are as firm as you like them; 2–3 minutes should do it for a runny poached egg. Using the slotted spoon, remove the eggs and transfer to a clean tea towel. Lightly dab the eggs with the towel to remove any excess water.

To serve, arrange two muffin or bagel halves on each plate and top with crispy bacon followed by a poached egg. Pour the hollandaise sauce over the eggs and garnish with a sprinkling of chives.

CHEF'S TIP

◆ If your hollandaise splits, immediately submerge the pan in ice-cold water and whisk in another egg yolk to bring the sauce back together.

SCRAMBLED EGG WITH PRAWNS AND BLACK PUDDING

◆◆◆

This may sound like an unusual combination of ingredients but I promise they work really well together. I came across a very similar dish while filming in Gran Canaria for TV3's Ireland AM, and this is my Irish version. Don't over-stir the scrambled egg. The eggs should have a very soft texture. Seasoning is really important. A nice variation is to add some Dijon mustard, cayenne pepper and chopped chives to the eggs. I served this as a starter at a wedding last year and out of the 200 guests, 150 ordered it. It's divine.

prep: 5 minutes ✦ **cook**: 14 minutes ✦ **serves**: 2

2 tbsp extra virgin olive oil

4 slices black pudding, about 2cm thick

50g butter

2 garlic cloves, peeled and finely chopped

½ red chilli, finely chopped

4 large prawns, peeled or not (as you prefer). See page 191 for instructions on how to devein prawns

FOR THE EGGS

4 free-range eggs

50ml cream

½ tsp ground nutmeg

¼ tsp sea salt and ¼ tsp freshly cracked black pepper

knob of butter

Add 1 tablespoon olive oil to a medium-sized frying pan over a medium heat and fry the black pudding for 1–2 minutes on each side. Then transfer, in the pan, into a warm oven set to 70°C fan/90°C/gas mark ¼, to keep warm.

In a separate shallow frying pan, gently heat the remaining olive oil and the butter. Add the garlic and chilli and cook gently to soften, but do not brown them. Add the prawns. Cook for about 3 minutes. If the prawns are not peeled they may need 5 minutes to cook, it really depends on the size. Remove the pan from the heat and transfer to the warm oven.

In a small bowl, whisk the eggs, cream and nutmeg, and season with salt and pepper. In a separate frying pan, add a knob of butter, and gradually combine the egg mixture into the pan and lightly scramble over a low heat, stirring continuously. This will take about 4 minutes.

Divide the egg mixture between two wide-rimmed bowls or plates and garnish with the black pudding and prawns.

Serve immediately.

◆◆◆

CHEF'S TIP

✦ Try not to overcook the eggs. Only ever cook 2 portions at a time, as otherwise you will crowd the pan with egg mixture and it won't work as well. You can also garnish with additional finely chopped fresh chilli and flat leaf parsley.

CURRIED SMOKED HADDOCK KEDGEREE

Kedgeree consists of flaked fish (usually smoked haddock), boiled rice, eggs and butter. The dish originated in colonial India, where fish caught in the early morning needed to be served quickly while it was still fresh, so the dish became a popular breakfast dish. You rarely see it served for breakfast now, but it makes a brilliant lunch. Another great feature of this dish is that it is made with mostly store-cupboard ingredients, so it's relatively frugal.

prep: 15 minutes ✦ **cook**: 20 minutes ✦ **serves**: 6

450g smoked haddock fillet

300ml milk

300ml double cream

1 tsp ground nutmeg

100g butter

1 tsp ground cumin

pinch of saffron, infused in 50ml water

1 tsp ground coriander

1 tsp curry powder

1 tsp turmeric

2 bay leaves

1 tsp black mustard seeds

1 tsp yellow mustard seeds

250g basmati rice

450ml vegetable or chicken stock

salt and freshly cracked black pepper

4 free-range eggs

2 spring onions, finely chopped

TO SERVE

2 tbsp chopped fresh coriander or chervil

4 wedges of lemon

samphire (optional)

Place the haddock in a saucepan with the milk, cream and nutmeg, and bring to a simmer. Cover and poach in the simmering liquid for 5 minutes. Remove the fish with a slotted spoon and allow to cool. Reserve the cooking liquid; it will keep in the fridge for up to 3 days and you can use it to make my classic fish pie (see recipe on page 208). When the fish is cool enough to handle, remove the skin and flake the flesh, carefully removing any bones. Sprinkle the haddock into your serving dish.

Melt the butter in a medium saucepan and add the cumin, saffron, ground coriander, curry powder, turmeric, bay leaves, mustard seeds and the rice. Sauté, stirring constantly, for 2 minutes. Pour in the stock and season with a pinch of salt and pepper. Bring to the boil and then reduce to simmer for about 10 minutes.

Meanwhile boil the eggs in a pan of water for 6 minutes. You want them not too soft in the centre, but to have a lovely bright yellow yolk that is creamy in texture. When the eggs are ready, run them under a cold tap and then peel and set aside to cool.

Stir the rice and add it to the haddock in the serving dish. Add the spring onions, slice the eggs in half and add to the dish. Season with salt and pepper once again, if required.

To serve, sprinkle the coriander or chervil over the top and serve with wedges of lemon and some delicious steamed samphire if you like.

PINTO BEAN SOUP (OR SAUTÉED PINTO BEANS)

◆◆◆

This recipe came about in a similar way to the one for black bean soup on page 127. I was preparing spicy pinto beans for a Mexican night in Medley and decided to try the same combination of ingredients and flavours to make a soup. It tastes great and has a sneaky kick of chilli.

prep: 5 minutes ✦ **cook**: 25–30 minutes ✦ **serves**: 4

1 tbsp sunflower or vegetable oil

2 onions, peeled and finely chopped

3 garlic cloves, finely chopped

2 green peppers, trimmed, deseeded and diced

2 tsp chopped fresh chilli

1 x 400g tin pinto beans, drained

3 tsp cumin seeds, toasted and crushed

2 tbsp dried oregano

1 litre vegetable stock

2 tsp freshly cracked black pepper

2 tsp salt

In a large pan, sauté the onions, garlic, peppers and chilli in the sunflower oil for 5 minutes. Then add the remaining ingredients, with 100ml of stock, into the pan and mix gently.

Bring to the boil and then reduce to a medium heat and cook for 20 minutes. Add the remaining stock, and cook over a medium heat for up to 10 minutes. Using a hand blender, blend the soup to your preferred consistency. Taste and season with more salt and pepper, if needed.

Serve with crusty bread.

◆◆◆

CHEF'S TIP

✦ To make pinto beans as an accompaniment for burritos, after sautéing the vegetables and adding the remaining ingredients (excluding the remaining stock), bring to the boil and then reduce to a medium heat for 20 minutes. Finally, reduce to a low simmer for 1 hour or until almost all the liquid has evaporated. Do leave a little moisture, however, as you don't want the beans to be too dry.

POTATO TORTILLA

Traditionally, Spanish omelettes are made with just potatoes, eggs, olive oil and salt. Occasionally onions are added to give extra flavour. There is no reason at all why you can't add tomato and ham or any other ingredient, of course. I visited a city called Ciudad Real, in Castile—La Mancha, and I couldn't believe that most cafés don't charge for tapas. I had the most stunning tortilla there and have endeavoured to recreate it here.

prep: 10 minutes ✦ **cook**: 30 minutes ✦ **serves**: 8–10

600g potatoes

2 tbsp olive oil

2 small onions, finely diced

3 garlic cloves, finely chopped

12 large free-range eggs

salt and freshly cracked black pepper

2 tsp ground nutmeg

2 tbsp cream

Peel and dice the potatoes. In a large saucepan, bring some salted water to the boil. Boil the potatoes for 5 minutes and then drain and cover.

While the potatoes are boiling, heat the olive oil in a large ovenproof frying pan. Lightly fry the onions and garlic until the onion is translucent but not brown. You want the onions to be soft and sweet. Remove from the heat and transfer the onion and garlic to a plate.

When the potatoes are ready, add a little oil to the pan and lightly fry the potatoes for about 5 minutes over a medium heat, until golden brown. Then add the onions and garlic back in and mix.

Preheat the oven to 180°C fan/200°C/gas mark 6.

Break the eggs into a bowl. Season with salt, pepper and nutmeg. Whisk lightly and add the cream. Pour the egg mixture over the potatoes and onions and cook over a low to medium heat. Using a small spatula, lift the egg mixture from time to time, especially around the sides to prevent it sticking. Continue cooking for 4–5 minutes until almost set.

Place the frying pan in the preheated oven and bake for about 20 minutes or until the egg is set (but still slightly soft to touch) and the top is golden brown. With a knife or small spatula, release the tortilla from the frying pan. Place a plate over the pan and flip over so that the tortilla comes out neatly onto the plate.

Serve immediately.

CHEF'S TIP

✦ It is really important to season the egg mixture very well before cooking. Simply taste with a teaspoon and adjust as required. This dish is lovely cold and my guilty pleasure is to serve it with a dollop of ketchup.

PORK TERRINE

◆◆◆

A terrine is a French forcemeat loaf similar to a pâté but made with more coarsely chopped ingredients. Terrines are usually served cold or at room temperature. This classic pork terrine is great served with chicken liver pâté (see recipe on page 97), some of Prue's treacle bread and my sweet chilli and red pepper jam (see recipe on page 166).

prep: 20 minutes ◆ **marinate**: 24 hours ◆ **cook**: 2 hours ◆ **serves**: 15

1 tbsp vegetable oil

4 shallots, peeled and finely chopped

3 garlic cloves, peeled and finely chopped

3 tbsp finely chopped fresh sage

3 tbsp finely chopped fresh tarragon

3 tbsp finely chopped fresh rosemary

400g rindless streaky rashers (approx 32 rashers)

500g boneless pork belly

200g pork fat

200g rindless back bacon

200g pork liver or lamb's liver

½ pork steak (tenderloin), finely diced

400g pork mince

2 free-range eggs

150ml white wine

100ml concentrated chicken stock or vegetable stock

2 tbsp freshly cracked black pepper

1 tbsp cumin seeds, dry roasted and crushed

2 tsp salt

1 tsp mixed spice

YOU WILL ALSO NEED

2 x 1 litre terrine moulds (or loaf tins), 18.5cm length x 9cm width x 6cm depth

Heat the oil in a frying pan over a medium heat and fry the shallots and garlic until softened but not browned. Add the sage, tarragon and rosemary. Fry for a further 2 minutes. Remove from the heat and transfer to a large mixing bowl.

Line 2 terrine moulds or loaf tins with the streaky rashers. Sizes vary, so use whatever you have.

Cut the pork belly, fat and back bacon into small pieces and blitz in a food processor. This will roughly mince the meat. Transfer to a mixing bowl. Cut the liver into thin strips and add to the mixing bowl.

Add the remaining ingredients to the mixing bowl and mix thoroughly. The diced pork steak will give the terrine a lovely texture. For best results, let the mixture stand, covered, in the fridge overnight, but this is optional. Transfer the mixture to the lined terrine moulds or baking tins. Press the mixture down with the back of a spoon so that it is well compacted. Smooth the surface and cover the moulds with tin foil.

Preheat the oven to 140°C fan/160°C/gas mark 3.

Place the terrines in a large roasting dish or ovenproof dish and pour in enough hot water to come three-quarters of the way up the sides. This is called a bain-marie and it allows the terrine to cook slowly and stay moist.

Cook for 1½ hours. Remove the tin foil and continue cooking for a further 30 minutes to brown the top of the terrine.

Remove from the oven and cover the terrines once again with foil or parchment paper and place a weight on the top of each one. This compresses the cooked mixture. Leave to cool and then refrigerate to set, overnight if you can.

Remove the terrine from the dish by carefully turning it out. Remove any excess liquid or fat and serve in slices with bread and a piquant relish.

CLASSIC FISH PIE

◆◆◆

A few years ago, I was asked to do a fish pie for a wedding I was catering. I played around with a few ideas and came up with this winning formula. It's simple to prepare, creamy in texture and above all delicious and wonderfully moreish.

prep: 40 minutes ✦ **chill**: 1 hour ✦ **cook**: 1 hour ✦ **serves**: 6–8

FOR THE PIE

1 small onion, thickly sliced

4 cloves

450ml milk

300ml double cream

450g cod fillet, skin on

225g smoked cod fillet (smoked haddock is great too)

½ tsp freshly grated nutmeg, plus a little extra

1 bay leaf

4 free-range eggs

70g butter

3 leeks, trimmed, washed and thinly sliced

70g plain flour

150ml white wine

1 fish stock cube

juice of ½ lemon

5 tbsp chopped fresh parsley

salt and freshly cracked black pepper

FOR THE MASH TOPPING

1.25kg floury potatoes, peeled

40g butter

1 free-range egg yolk

pinch freshly grated nutmeg

Stud a couple of the onion slices with cloves. Put the onion slices in a large pan with the milk, cream, cod, smoked cod, nutmeg and bay leaf. Bring the heat up until the liquid is just about to boil, and then reduce the heat and leave to simmer over a low heat for 8 minutes. The fish should be opaque and tender.

Lift the fish out with a slotted spoon and transfer to a plate. Strain the cooking liquid (stock) into a jug and discard the onions. When the fish is cool enough to handle, break it into large flakes, discarding the skin and bones. Transfer the fish to a shallow rectangular ovenproof dish.

Boil the eggs for just 8 minutes, then drain and leave to cool. Peel and cut them into chunky slices and arrange the slices on top of the fish.

Melt the butter in a large saucepan, add the leeks and sauté gently for 5 minutes, until soft. Add the flour and cook for 1 minute. Take the pan off the heat and gradually stir in the wine, the stock cube and the reserved cooking stock from the fish. Return the pan to the heat and slowly bring to the boil, stirring all the time. Add the lemon juice and allow to simmer gently for 10 minutes, to cook the flour. Remove from the heat once more, stir in the parsley, taste, and season with nutmeg, salt and black pepper. Pour the sauce over the fish and leave to cool. Cover and refrigerate for 1 hour.

Meanwhile boil the potatoes for 15–20 minutes. Drain and mash with the butter and egg yolk. Season with a pinch of nutmeg and freshly ground salt and pepper. Beat in just enough milk to form a soft, spreadable mash. You can also reserve some of the stock from poaching the fish to use for this.

Preheat the oven to 180°C fan/200°C/gas mark 6.

Remove the fish pie from the fridge and spoon or pipe the mashed potato over the top. Draw a fork gently along the mashed

salt and freshly cracked black pepper

150ml milk

150g grated Cheddar cheese (red or white)

YOU WILL ALSO NEED

1 x shallow ovenproof dish, approximately
   30cm x 24cm

potato top to create a textured surface (this will help to make it lovely and crispy), sprinkle with the cheese, and bake for 35–40 minutes, until piping hot and golden brown.

❖❖❖

CHEF'S TIP

✦ You could add some chopped fresh dill to this dish if you like. I also like to add smoked salmon, prawns and 15–20 cherry tomatoes sometimes. Just sprinkle the tomatoes over the white sauce, before you top with the mash.

CHICKEN WITH OLIVES AND MASCARPONE

When I was devising a new Italian menu recently for Medley, I didn't want to churn out the same old Italian dishes, but at the same time I wanted to use classic Italian flavours and ingredients. The olive oil marinade in this dish helps to keep the chicken so tender and moist in the oven that it's as if the chicken steams while cooking. The result is magic.

prep: 20 minutes ✦ **marinate**: 30 minutes or overnight ✦ **cook**: 35 minutes ✦ **serves**: 4

FOR THE CHICKEN

4 chicken supremes

150ml extra virgin olive oil

2 tbsp chopped fresh rosemary

salt and freshly cracked black pepper, to taste

FOR THE SAUCE

2 tbsp sunflower oil

1 medium onion, finely chopped

3 garlic cloves, finely chopped

1 tsp hot chilli powder or chilli flakes

1 tbsp chopped fresh rosemary

1 tbsp chopped curly parsley

salt and freshly cracked black pepper

2 x 400g tins chopped tomatoes

1 tsp sugar

150ml red wine

250ml mascarpone cheese

100g green olives, pitted and chopped (or left whole)

In a food processor, prepare the marinade by blending the olive oil, rosemary, salt and pepper. Place the chicken supremes into a bowl with the marinade, making sure that the chicken is well coated. Cover and refrigerate for a minimum of 30 minutes but overnight if you can.

Preheat the oven to 180°C fan/200°C/gas mark 6. Place the chicken in an ovenproof dish and bake in the hot oven for 20–35 minutes or until cooked through. Set aside.

While the chicken is baking, prepare the sauce. Heat the oil in a pan and add the onion, garlic, chilli, rosemary and parsley and lightly sauté for 5 minutes over a low heat. Season with salt and pepper. Add the tomatoes, sugar and wine. Bring to the boil and then reduce the heat and simmer gently for 10 minutes. Using a hand blender, blend until smooth. Taste and season with salt and pepper, if necessary. Remove about 100ml of the tomato sauce to a Pyrex jug or similar and fold in the mascarpone cheese. Then gradually add this creamy mixture back into the tomato sauce, mixing gently as you go, taking care that the mascarpone does not split. Finally, add the olives.

Serve the chicken on warm plates with the tomato sauce poured over and a mixed bean salad or green salad on the side.

CHEF'S TIPS

✦ Adding red wine to a tomato sauce greatly improves the depth of flavour.

✦ Adding sugar counteracts the acidity of tinned tomatoes.

RACK OF LAMB WITH GARLIC AND ROSEMARY AND A PEPPER CRUST

This is an impressive dish but it really does need to be cooked medium rare. It is simple to prepare and rather elegant when presented on a large serving platter. Ask your butcher to prepare a French-trimmed rack of lamb. This dish also works really well with the mint and coriander salsa (see page 31).

prep: 1 hour ✦ **marinate**: 2–24 hours ✦ **cook**: 18 minutes ✦ **serves**: 8

FOR THE LAMB

4 racks of lamb (2 pairs of best ends, French trimmed)

50ml olive oil

6 garlic whole cloves, skin on

4 sprigs of fresh rosemary

FOR THE PEPPER CRUST

2 tbsp peppercorns

2 tbsp coriander seeds

1 tbsp rock salt

bunch of fresh thyme

FOR THE JUS

2 shallots, peeled and finely diced

1 tbsp chopped fresh rosemary

2 garlic cloves, crushed

100g cold, unsalted butter, cubed

salt and freshly cracked black pepper

500ml concentrated chicken stock

1 tbsp balsamic vinegar

150ml Madeira wine or red wine

To prepare the lamb, trim the fillet to remove any sinew, outer layers of fat or white membrane.

In a large pan, dry fry the peppercorns and coriander seeds for the pepper crust. You just want to toast them gently to release their flavour. Be careful not to burn them or to allow the pan to smoke. Remove them from the heat and crush with a pestle and mortar. Then add the salt and thyme and mix well. Spread the mixture out on a flat tray.

Pour the olive oil into a flat dish. Roll the lamb (loin end) in the olive oil and then roll it in the pepper crust mixture. Continue until the lamb is evenly covered in a thin layer of spice crust. Tightly wrap the crusted loin end in cling film and then in tin foil. Place in the fridge overnight or for a minimum of 2 hours. Make sure to remove the lamb from the fridge at least one hour before you are going to cook it, to allow it to come back up to room temperature.

To prepare the jus, sauté the shallots, rosemary and garlic in 50g of the butter. Season with salt and pepper. Add the stock, balsamic vinegar and Madeira wine, bring up to the boil and then reduce to a simmer. Let the jus gently simmer until the liquid has reduced in volume by half. Remove from the heat. Check the seasoning and add more if needed.

Preheat the oven to 200°C fan/220°C/gas mark 7.

To cook the lamb, heat a non-stick frying pan with a little vegetable oil in it. When it is very hot, add the lamb (loin end) and sear it on all sides for 1½–2 minutes on each side until evenly browned all over. Place in a roasting tin and scatter with the whole garlic cloves and sprigs of rosemary.

Place the roasting tin in the oven for 18 minutes for medium

CHEF'S TIP

+ You can also strain the jus to remove the shallots and garlic if you like. Personally, I prefer the texture of the jus with the finely-chopped shallots. You can also thicken the jus with a roux if you like (see page 138 for instructions).

rare. Remove from the oven. Cover with a damp tea towel and then tin foil and allow to rest in a warm oven (65–70°C) for at least 5 minutes before carving.

After the lamb has been cooked, strain the meat juices from the pan into the jus. Then gently heat the gravy and whisk in the remaining 50g of cubed butter, until the butter is melted. Set aside for 5 minutes and then scoop off any fatty residue from the top of the jus.

To serve, carve into cutlets, and serve with a selection of seasonal vegetables. Drizzle the jus over the lamb cutlets.

BRAISED CABBAGE WITH BACON LARDONS

My chef Paul and I were devising a seven-course French tasting menu recently for Bastille Day. I wanted to do something completely different to complement the fillet of beef main course. Inspiration came from a Roux brothers recipe and a recent holiday in Provence. I love this dish — it's beautifully simple and incredibly tasty.

prep: 10 minutes ✦ **cook**: 30 minutes ✦ **serves**: 4–6

1 head of savoy cabbage (about 2kg), core removed and finely shredded

1 tbsp extra virgin olive oil

2 tbsp butter

250g bacon lardons

2 banana shallots, peeled and finely diced

3 garlic cloves, diced

500ml chicken stock (or vegetable)

salt and freshly cracked black pepper to taste

Preheat the oven to 180°C fan/200°C/gas mark 6.

Fill a large saucepan with water and bring to the boil. Place the shredded cabbage into the boiling water, reduce the heat and simmer for 3 minutes. Drain in a colander and immediately place the cabbage in ice-cold water to stop it from cooking any further. Drain again after 2 minutes and then place in a casserole dish.

Gently heat half the olive oil and butter in a frying pan. Fry the bacon lardons until crispy. Transfer the crispy lardons to the bed of cabbage.

In the same frying pan, heat the remaining oil and butter, and gently sauté the shallots and garlic for 5 minutes or until the shallots are soft and translucent. Season with salt and pepper. Transfer to the bed of cabbage and bacon lardons. Add the stock and mix well. Cover with tin foil and place in the preheated oven for 30 minutes. Mix again. Taste and check for seasoning.

Transfer to a serving platter and serve immediately.

CHEF'S TIPS

✦ Blanching the cabbage in ice-cold water not only stops it from overcooking but will also maintain the vibrant green colour.

✦ If you are serving individual portions, you will need to drain the cooked cabbage; otherwise there will be too much liquid on the plate.

BRAISED OXTAIL STEW

———— ◆◆◆ ————

Oxtail is a bony, gelatin-rich cut of meat that is usually slow cooked as a stew or braised. This cut is also used for the stock base of oxtail soup. The robust beef flavour of this dish comes from the bones and marrow, but the meat is also very tasty. This oxtail stew recipe is typically Spanish. I was in Madrid during the Dos de Mayo festival season a few years ago and that was when I enjoyed my very first oxtail stew.

prep: 1 hour ◆ **marinate**: 24 hours ◆ **cook**: 3 hours ◆ **serves**: 8–10

FOR THE MARINADE

750ml (1 bottle) good red wine (typically a Rioja)

2.5kg oxtail, cut into 5cm chunks

2 carrots, peeled and sliced in three

2 celery stalks, peeled and sliced into batons

2 large onions, roughly chopped

3 garlic cloves, peeled but left whole

bouquet garni, to include 2 bay leaves, parsley stalks, 6 sprigs of thyme, sprig of rosemary

FOR THE STEW

4 tbsp plain flour

2 tsp smoked paprika

salt and freshly cracked black pepper

a little sunflower oil, for frying

100g butter

sprig of fresh thyme

2 tbsp tomato purée

2 x 400g tins of chopped tomatoes

1 litre of beef stock

TO SERVE

handful of fresh parsley, chopped

creamy mash (optional)

To marinate the oxtail, heat a heavy casserole pot, bring the wine to the boil and reduce by one-third. This will remove the alcohol and concentrate the colour and flavour. Leave to cool. In a large bowl, mix the oxtail pieces, carrot, celery, onion, garlic and bouquet garni and pour the cooled red wine over them. Cover and marinate in the fridge for 24 hours.

The next day, drain the oxtail pieces and vegetables but reserve the liquid. Pat the oxtail pieces dry with kitchen paper.

Preheat the oven to 200°C fan/220°C/gas mark 7. Place the 4 tablespoons of flour on a baking tray and toast in the hot oven for 10 minutes. Remove and allow to cool.

Season the flour with the paprika, salt and pepper, then toss the oxtail in it until evenly coated. Heat the oil in a large heatproof casserole dish. Working in batches, brown the oxtail really well on all sides. This will take about 5 minutes. Remove from the dish and transfer to a baking tray. Place in the oven for 30 minutes.

In the meantime, deglaze the pan with 150ml of the retained marinade liquid, and then add the butter, drained vegetables and bouquet garni and fry for 3–4 minutes until everything starts to colour. Stir in the tomato purée and tinned tomatoes. Remove the oxtails from the oven and tip the meat back into the casserole dish. Pour over the remaining marinade and then the stock. You may need to add more wine (150ml) and stock (500ml) to cover the stew. This really depends on the size of your casserole dish. Bring to the boil and cook for 5 minutes. Remove from the heat.

Then reduce the oven to 160°C fan/180°C/gas mark 4.

Season again, if required, and then cover the casserole dish and braise in the oven for 3 hours, until the meat is meltingly tender.

Serve with creamy mash (see recipe on page 98).

CINNAMON APPLE AND RHUBARB CRUMBLE

❖❖❖

This dish takes me back to my schooldays at Wilson's Hospital School in Multyfarnham, County Westmeath. A group of friends and I were asked to dinner with our headmaster, Robert Whiteside. He made a rhubarb crumble for dessert and it was delicious. It has been one of my favourite desserts ever since and I wanted to create my own version and dedicate it to him.

prep: 5 minutes ✦ **cook**: 40–45 minutes ✦ **serves**: 6–8

FOR THE FRUIT BASE

5 large cooking apples, peeled, cored and sliced

5 stalks of rhubarb, washed, peeled and cut into 2cm pieces

100g butter

4 tbsp brown sugar

juice of ½ orange

50ml liqueur of your choice

zest of 1 orange

FOR THE CRUMBLE TOPPING

150g cold butter, cut into cubes

100g plain flour

100g wholemeal flour

1 tsp salt

150g porridge oats

150g brown sugar

30g walnuts, shelled and chopped (optional)

1 tbsp ground cinnamon

TO SERVE

softly whipped cream or ice cream (optional)

YOU WILL ALSO NEED

25cm x 16cm deep ovenproof dish

Preheat the oven to 160°C fan/180°C/gas mark 4.

In a large frying pan, lightly fry the apple and rhubarb pieces in the butter. Sprinkle over the brown sugar and, once the fruit is lightly caramelised, add the orange juice, liqueur and zest and stir well. Then transfer the fruit to an ovenproof baking dish and allow to cool slightly while you make the crumble topping.

To make the crumble, place the chilled, cubed butter in a large bowl and sieve in the plain flour. Add the wholemeal flour and the salt. Rub the butter into the flour until the mixture resembles breadcrumbs. Then add in the oats, sugar, walnuts and cinnamon and mix well.

Sprinkle the crumble topping over the fruit and bake in the preheated oven for 40–45 minutes.

Serve with softly whipped cream or vanilla ice cream.

❖❖❖

CHEF'S TIP

✦ A great way to remove the tough strings of the rhubarb is to peel it with a vegetable peeler. If there is too much crumble topping, you can store this in a ziplock bag or airtight container for use another time.

CHOCOLATE AMARETTO BREAD AND BUTTER PUDDING

✦✦✦

This is one of the easiest puddings to make. It's a great way to use up leftover bread, whether white or brown. I don't use raisins, but if you like you can add about 150g raisins or sultanas by simply sprinkling them over the bread before pouring the chocolate custard. This is an adult dessert as it contains booze, but you can of course leave it out if you're looking for a more family-friendly version.

prep: 20 minutes ✦ **cook**: 30–40 minutes ✦ **serves**: 6–8

100g dark chocolate (70 per cent cocoa solids)

200g butter, cubed and softened

1 sliced white pan (800g), crusts removed

2 tbsp water

2 whole free-range eggs

3 free-range egg yolks

250ml milk

150ml double cream

4 tsp amaretto liqueur

2 tsp vanilla extract

50g caster sugar, plus a little extra

35ml dark rum

a pinch of salt

75g pack of amaretti biscuits, whole

YOU WILL ALSO NEED

1 x oval ovenproof dish, approximately 30cm x 20cm.

──── ✦✦✦ ────

CHEF'S TIP

✦ Bread and butter pudding reheats really well. Just cover with tin foil and heat in a hot oven for about 20 minutes. You can also season with freshly ground nutmeg.

Preheat the oven to 160°C fan/180°C/gas mark 4. Lightly butter the ovenproof dish.

To prepare the melted chocolate, break the chocolate into pieces and place them in a Pyrex or similar heatproof bowl with the cubed butter. Fill a saucepan with an inch or so of water, bring up to a gentle simmer and place the bowl over it, making sure the bottom of the bowl does not touch the hot water. This is a bain-marie. Over a low heat, allow the steam from the simmering water to melt the contents of the bowl gently. Once melted, remove from the heat immediately.

While the chocolate is melting, cut each slice of bread in half and butter both sides. Once the chocolate has melted, mix in 2 tablespoons of water very slowly to produce a creamy texture.

In a separate bowl mix the eggs, egg yolks, milk, cream, amaretto liqueur, vanilla extract, melted chocolate and caster sugar. Stir in the rum and salt.

Line your dish with the buttered bread slices, letting them overlap each other a little. Layer the amaretti biscuits over the bread. Carefully pour the chocolate mixture over the bread and biscuit layers. Continue with a second layer of bread, biscuit and chocolate mixture until all are used up. Give the mixure a gentle press with your fingers so that the bread is totally submerged in the chocolate custard. Leave for 30 minutes or more so that the bread will soak up the liquid. Lightly sprinkle a little extra caster sugar over the top and bake in the oven for 30–40 minutes or until just set.

Serve warm rather than hot, with lashings of thick cream.

MERINGUE ROULADE

A meringue roulade is quick and easy to make and always proves very popular with guests. It's perfect for an al fresco party in summer or even on Christmas Day. People tend to be intimidated as the rolling looks complicated. In fact it couldn't be easier. The ingredients are inexpensive, so why not practise so that you can get it perfect?

prep: 15 minutes ✦ **cook**: 23 minutes ✦ **serves**: 6–8

4 free-range egg whites

225g caster sugar

TO SERVE

250ml whipped cream

strawberries, raspberries or fresh fruit of
 your choice

fresh mint leaves

icing sugar, to dust

YOU WILL ALSO NEED

32cm x 20cm Swiss roll tin

Preheat the oven to 165°C fan/185°C/gas mark 4.

Line the Swiss roll tin with tin foil and brush lightly with sunflower or vegetable oil, which won't affect the flavour. This prevents the meringue from sticking.

In a clean, dry bowl, beat the egg whites a little and then add the sugar and whisk until the mixture forms stiff peaks. Spread the meringue gently into the lined tin with a palette knife. It should be thick and quite bouncy.

Bake in the preheated oven for 23 minutes. Remove from the oven and set aside to cool.

Put another sheet of tin foil on the work surface and turn out the meringue onto it, meringue side down. Carefully peel off the tin foil from the cooked meringue base. Allow to cool.

To assemble, spread the whipped cream over the roulade. Reserve some to pipe on top. Cover with a layer of fruit of your choice and roll like a Swiss roll.

Carefully transfer to a serving dish. Using a piping bag, pipe some rosettes of cream on the top and garnish with fruit and fresh mint leaves. Dredge with icing sugar.

Serve immediately or refrigerate until ready to serve.

CHEF'S TIPS

✦ Ensure that the oven is up to temperature before cooking the meringue.

✦ Make sure the bowl is clean, dry and dust-free before whisking the egg whites.